Sculpture
in
Paper

Red Groomes, *Dali Salad,* 1980–81. Paper,
mixed media, 26½ x 27½ x 12½" (67 x 70 x
32 cm), edition of 55. Courtesy Brooke
Alexander Gallery, New York.

SCULPTURE
IN
PAPER

Nicholas Roukes

Davis Publications, Inc.
Worcester, Massachusetts

For Julie

Acknowledgements

The author is grateful to the artists, museums and galleries that have provided information and visual material for this book. Special thanks go to Sheril Cunning, Jean LaPointe Mihalcheon, Chuck Hilger, John Babcock, Dorothea Eimert, Elisabeth Sinken, Franz Zeier, Bob Stowell, Ken Samuelson, Peter Pfenning, Brian N. Queen, Kathy Johnson, Marc J. Beeger, Christine Greco and Lilian A. Bell. A thank-you is also extended to the students of the Alberta College of Art who have contributed visual material. As always, extra special thanks to Julie Roukes, for help in reading the manuscript and providing constructive criticism during research and production.

Editor: Martha Siegel
Design: Douglass Scott and Diane Bigda

Type set in Minion and Univers Condensed by Glassman/Mayerchak

Library of Congress Catalog Card Number: 92-072329
ISBN: 87192-246-0
10 9 8 7 6 5 4 3 2

Cover: Carolyn Dahl, *Pleated Rhythms*,
1989. Dyed, pleated paper, 11 x 17 x 17"
(28 x 43 x 43 cm). Courtesy the artist.

Contents

Preface

Paper—a natural material made from cellulose found in plant fibers—has been man's faithful servant for over 2,000 years. As an art medium it is flexible, easy to handle, inexpensive and nontoxic. Above all, it holds an enormous potential that awaits the artist's sympathetic touch. Although modern technology continues to materialize new products at a dizzying pace, paper remains indispensable as a vehicle for facilitating and revealing human thought and endeavor.

Curiously, artists worldwide have only in this century come to appreciate the intrinsic qualities of paper as a fine art medium, having used it heretofore mainly as a substratum—a material upon which expression is placed. Notable exceptions are found in the history of arts and crafts from various cultural and ethnic groups. However, only since the advent of collage, introduced by Georges Braque and Pablo Picasso in the early 1900s, has paper truly come into its own as an autonomous fine art medium.

The purpose of *Sculpture in Paper* is to acquaint you with creative manifestations, expressions, techniques and ideas. The material in this book is intended for either personal or classroom use by the student, professional or "Sunday artist." The chapter entitled *Portfolio: Across Boundaries* presents a showcase of works in paper sculpture created by contemporary artists from many parts of the world. Within the ensuing pages of this book you'll find a brief history of paper, a description of how paper is made and technical information describing the various qualities and types of papers. You will also find directions for methods of manipulating and fashioning paper into artforms, including cut-paper designs, abstract and figurative constructions, collage and papier-mâché. Although the emphasis is on the use of commercially fabricated paper, there is also information dealing with basic hand-papermaking techniques that employ ready-to-use pulp and commonplace appliances such as the kitchen blender. The bibliography at the end of this book comprises publications for further research.

I invite you to join the artists who have rediscovered paper, a user-friendly material that—when treated with respect and imagination—will transform almost magically from a flat, inanimate substance into one charged with imagery and dynamic form.

—N.R. Calgary, Alberta, Canada

Vito Capone, *Stratificato,* 1985. Sculpted paper, 7 x 7" (18 x 18 cm). Courtesy the artist. Photograph by Gianfranco Gesmundo.

Opposite:
Elisabeth Sinken, *Objects 8.* Paper construction. Courtesy the artist.

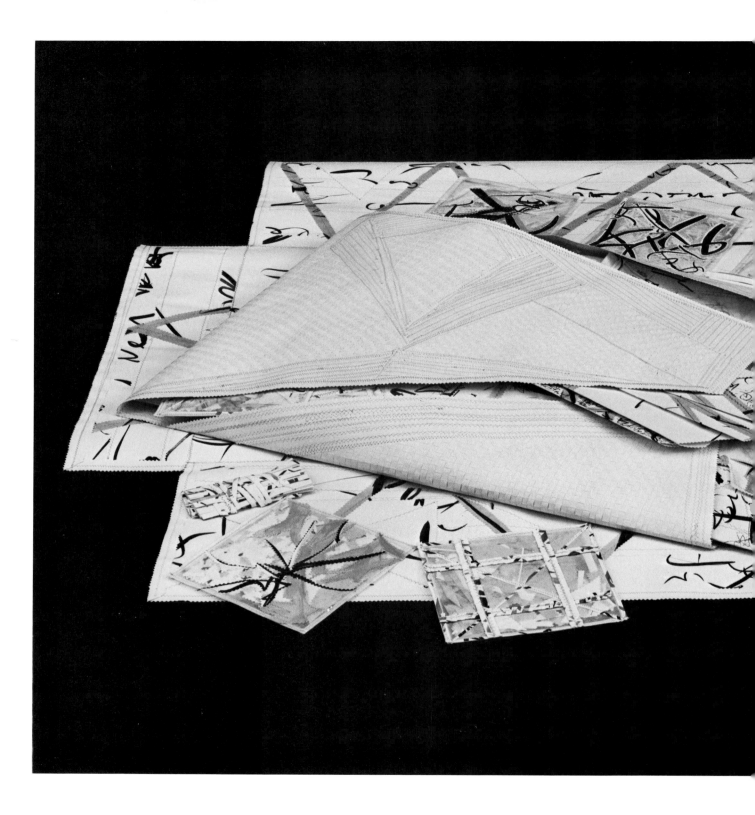

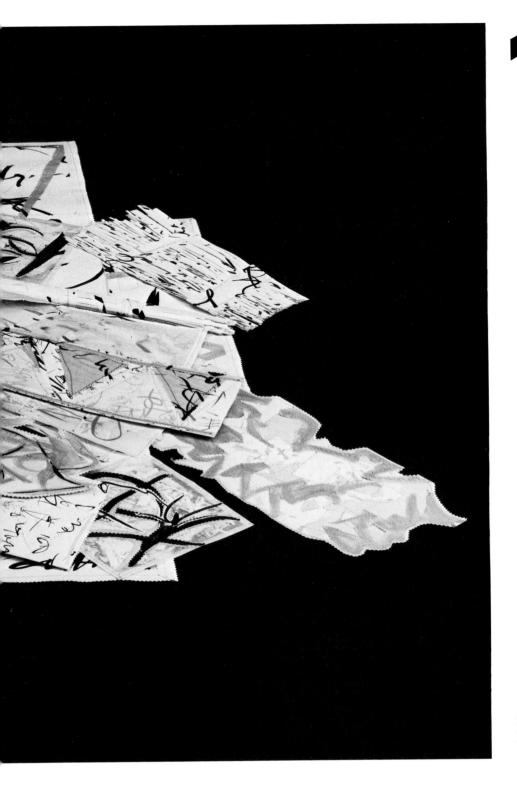

1

An Old/New Medium

Lise Landry, *J'ecris Pour Vous Dire*, 1983.
Japanese paper, mixed media, 52 x 65"
(132 x 164 cm). Courtesy the artist.

The invention of paper is credited to the Chinese and heralded as an epic event in world history. It seems that Ts'ai Lun—an imperial guard in the Chinese emperor's court—invented paper in A.D. 105 as a substitute for materials such as papyrus, silk, bamboo slip, parchment and vellum, which were previously used as writing surfaces. Before paper was invented, almost every conceivable material was used as a writing, drawing or painting surface. Materials included clay, bone, wood, stone, palm leaves, tapa, cloth and even metal. Although historical records indicate that the Egyptians used papyrus as a writing surface, the Egyptians did not break the plant down into separate fibers, as did Ts'ai Lun, to produce true paper.

It should be noted, however, that even before Ts'ai Lun's legendary discovery, paper was being manufactured and used on this planet by an industrious creature of nature: the common wasp. This tiny powerhouse instinctively uses its sharp teeth to gnaw, pound and knead water-soaked wood filaments into pulp. It binds the pulp with a sticky secretion from its body and spreads the resultant paste in thin layers to produce paper for building its nest. Perhaps it was this spectacle of nature that inspired Ts'ai Lun to invent paper.

As the practice of papermaking spread throughout the civilized world, each country's artisans adapted indigenous materials for production. In Korea and other Asian countries, pulp was prepared from fibers of hemp, rattan, bamboo, rice straw, seaweed and mulberry bark. At the same time, in Europe and other countries in the Western hemisphere, linen and cotton fibers were used to make

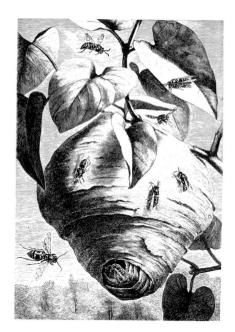

Wasps at their Nest. **Courtesy Dover Publications, New York.**

The Journey of Papermaking. **Courtesy Dover Publications, New York.**

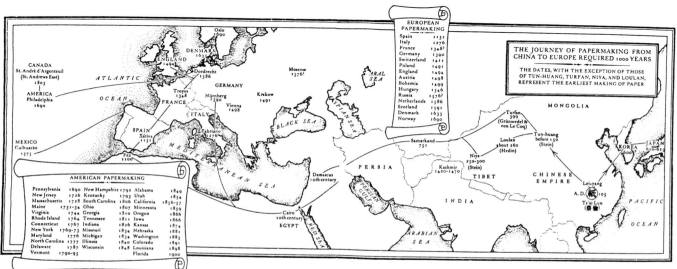

pulp. Today, cotton and linen remain the principle materials in fine quality papers, but the most commonly used substance in commercial papermaking is wood pulp.

Papermaking wended its way westward from China, through Central Asia and Persia along the route that eventually came to be known as the Silk Road. Virgin flax fibers were used in the Islamic world to produce pulp that was made into many types of decorative papers. It appears that papermaking came to Europe by way of Spain in the tenth century, with activity centering around Cordova and Seville. From Spain, papermaking migrated to Italy, France and Germany. The first papermaking mill in North America was established in 1690 in Germantown, near Philadelphia.

Inventions and Innovations

Among the inventions that prompted increased paper production were the printing press of Johannes Gutenberg in the 1400s in Germany, the Hollander beater in the mid-seventeenth century in the Netherlands (a device that provided an efficient method for macerating rags) and the papermaking machine of Nicholas-Louis Robert in the early 1800s in France. A different type of paper-making apparatus—the cylinder machine or mold machine—was developed in England by John Dickinson in 1809. Thomas Gilpin set up a cylinder machine at his Delaware mill in 1817 and is credited with producing the first machine-made paper in the United States.

Despite these innovations, the basic way of making paper, whether by hand or machine, has remained virtually unchanged for over 2,000 years.

Classifications of Paper

Paper can be classified in three categories according to production methods: machine-made, mold-made and handmade. Machine-made paper, such as newsprint, is manufactured in large volume by paper mills using a Fourdrinier. This giant machine can run at speeds of 3,500 feet per minute producing a continuous roll of paper 30 feet wide. It makes the paper on a fast-moving belt of woven-wire mesh, transfers it to a felt, expresses the moisture, dries the paper and finally rolls the paper up at the end of its production line.

Finer quality mold-made paper is produced in more limited quantity on the cylinder machine, a device similar to John Dickinson's invention of the early nineteenth century. Here, the web is formed on the surface of a wire-covered

Seventeenth century papermaking in Europe. The vatman is shown plunging a mold into the paper pulp (known as slurry) while helpers deposit sheets of the freshly-made paper between pieces of felt. The slurry is kept warm by a charcoal-fired heater known as a pistolet (shown at far left), a device which increased the speed of production. Mechanical stamping mills (background right) macerated cotton fiber in preparation for papermaking. Anonymous, *Papermakers*, circa 1700. Woodcut. Courtesy Dover Publications, New York.

Making paper is truly a hands-on activity. Kathyrn Clark, American papermaker, producing a sheet of paper from a mold and deckle. Courtesy the artist and Twinrocker, Inc.

cylinder that revolves in a vat of pulp. The cylinder is subsequently transferred to a moving felt.

Handmade paper is the most labor-intensive of all to produce because each sheet is individually made by the artisan. Today, handmade papers are produced in much the same manner as they were in ancient times. Each sheet is made with a screen mold and deckle, which is a two-part, finely-meshed frame. The screen mold and deckle is plunged deep into a vat of wet pulp and removed to trap a thin layer of fibers, which become interlocked. The deckle is a wooden frame that fits on top of the screen mold and serves to control the dimensions of the pulp.

"To be classified as a true paper," wrote Dard Hunter, the principle force and historian in American papermaking, "the thin sheets must be made from fiber that has been macerated until each individual filament is a separate unit; the fibers lifted from the water in the form of a thin stratum, the water draining through the small openings of the screen leaving a sheet of matted fiber upon the screen's surface."

The matted pulp is subsequently removed from the mold and deckle, transferred to a dampened felt, compressed and dried. It then becomes a sheet of paper.

The attractive handmade papers of Japan, called washi, are made from plant fibers such as kozo, mitsumata and gampi. The process follows an ancient, time-honored tradition. Branches from the plants are cut and steamed, and the outer bark is removed. The inner bark is then cooked in an alkaline solution until fibers separate easily. The rinsed and cleaned fibers are then beaten with hardwood rods or mallets for final breakdown. (Mechanical beaters such as the Hollander machine are used by contemporary Japanese craftsworkers for faster production.) The pulp is then stirred into a vat of water in about a one-to-two ratio and agitated with a comb-like rake to blend. Neri, a starchy mucilage that looks like egg white, is mixed into the solution. This prevents clumping, allowing fibers to float evenly.

To make individual sheets of paper, the artist plunges a screen mold and deckle into the vat and scoops up the pulpy solution. The artist then skillfully shakes and tosses the solution on the screen, causing fibers to cross and cohere on the surface while the water drains through. Papermakers liken this tossing to waves of the sea, because the rocking motion and sound of pulp is reminiscent of the ocean's action.

The dipping process is repeated until the desired thickness is achieved. The Japanese paper sheet is made up of multiple layers of pulp, produced by three or more dippings.

The dipping screen is removed from the deckle and placed paper-side down onto a board. The screen is pulled away, allowing the paper to remain on the cloth. This process is repeated, and each newly-molded sheet is placed over the last. The stack of sheets is allowed to rest overnight before being placed in a screw or hydraulic press. Gentle pressure is administered slowly over a period of hours. Finally, after pressing, the sheets are separated and brushed onto boards to dry.

Although rewarding, producing handmade paper from raw material is time-consuming, wet and laborious. It's no wonder that an anonymous papermaker once lamented, "Heaven does not permit such a divine art to be made easy for mortals here below."

A shortcut to papermaking involves ready-to-use pulp, known as linter, which is packaged either in chip form in gallon containers or as dry sheets. The prepared pulp is rehydrated using a kitchen blender or hydropulper.

paper/pā´-pər/n: A substance composed of fibers interlaced into a compact web, made usually in the form of a thin flexible sheet, most commonly white, from various fibrous materials, such as linen and cotton rags, straw, wood, certain grasses, etc., which are macerated into a pulp, dried, and pressed.

OXFORD ENGLISH DICTIONARY, 2ND EDITION, 1989.

Artistry in Paper

Paper escaped from its role as a "substrata" medium in the early 1900s with the advent of collage by Cubist artists such as Pablo Picasso, Georges Braque, Juan Gris and Kurt Schwitters. Rather than drawing and painting shapes and textures in photographic-like realism, in the trompe l'oeil tradition, collage artists opted to paste actual textured materials on their canvasses. This innovation forced pictorial composition into the world of objects.

The French poet Guillaume Apollinaire summed up the iconoclastic spirit of these pioneer artists when he wrote, "You may now paint with whatever materi-

Pablo Picasso, *Guitar,* 1913. Cut-and-pasted paper, ink, charcoal and white chalk on blue paper, mounted on board, 26⅛ x 19½" (66 x 50 cm). Courtesy The Museum of Modern Art, New York. Nelson A. Rockefeller Bequest.

al you please: with pipes, postage stamps, postcards, playing cards, pieces of oil-cloth, collars, painted paper or newspapers."

The Cubist collage artists were the first to exploit paper as a sculptural medium. They employed methods such as cutting, creasing, scoring, folding, rolling, crumpling, embossing, punching, piercing, tearing, fraying, scratching, singeing, gluing and decorating to discover the expressive potential of the material. They found paper eminently suitable for experiments in mixed media, collage, decoupage and assemblage. Later, in 1959, the American artist Robert Rauschenberg created a series of paintings he dubbed "combines," a mixed-media in which paper, miscellaneous materials and "found objects" (those found in the environment) were united in a single art form. Rauschenberg, explaining his departure from traditional approaches to art, said, "I'm trying to check my habits of seeing, trying to become *unfamiliar* with what I'm doing."

The German Bauhaus academy was an influential precursor to our present school system art curricula. From 1925 to 1928, a preliminary course at the Bauhaus taught by Josef Albers held as its objective, "The education of the student towards sensitivity of architectural and visual experience." In Albers' design course, students worked chiefly with paper and scissors to investigate the expressive potential of paper, the interaction of form and space and the phenomenon of optical illusion.

As writer Jasia Reichardt observes, contemporary art expression in paper stems from three distinct strands of activity: printmaking, from which artists have expanded techniques to include sculptural uses of paper and pulp; paper-folding and -cutting, with precedents in Asian and European paper cuts, origami and cardboard construction; and papier-mâché and decollage, under the aegis of Cubist collage and assemblage.

Contemporary expression in paper also originates from the orbit of sculpture itself, wherein a new fascination with this old/new medium appears to have materialized.

Pablo Picasso, *Violin,* 1912-13. Cardboard and string, 23 x 9½ x 3" (58 x 24 x 8 cm). Courtesy Staatsgalerie, Stuttgart.

Henri Matisse, *Polynesia (The Sky)*, 1946.
Cut paper, 76¾ x 12½" (200 x 32 cm).
Courtesy Centre National d'Art et de
Culture George Pompidou, Musee
National d'art Moderne, Paris.

Anonymous, *Divine Creature Bearing
Young Child,* late Ching dynasty. Paper
cut, 9 x 12" (23 x 30 cm). Courtesy Eddie
Lui.

Attributed to contemporary Greek puppeteer Spiropoulos. Shadow Puppet Serpent.

Teizo Hashimoto, Japanese Edo kite, contemporary. Handpainted paper. Courtesy Tal Streeter, *The Art of the Japanese Kite,* John Wetherhill Publishers.

There is a belief in parts of China that if you pierce a piece of paper with many minute perforations, and then sacrifice it by setting it on fire, any demon who happens to be about at the time will be forced to jump through each pinhole before the fire reaches it, thus completely losing face.

CARSON I.A. RITCHIE, WRITER

Matsutaro Yanase, *Footman Kite,*
contemporary. Wash drawing on paper.
Courtesy Tal Streeter, *The Art of the
Japanese Kite,* John Wetherhill
Publishers.

Paper as Craft

Paper has its oldest and richest heritage in the category of crafts. The art of
paper-folding, for example, dates back to China before the sixth century. Paper-
folding later emerged in Japan and Korea, where it eventually became known as
origami. Before origami became a popular craft idiom, it served in religious and
ceremonial rites. Paper constructions called sembra zuru (a thousand cranes)
were commonly offered as a silent prayer in Japanese shrines.

Chinese artisans also used paper sculpture in ceremonial rites. Paper was considered a sacred material. The color of paper—white—was the color of mourn-
ing as well as immortality. There are accounts of full-size paper figures, animals,
sedan chairs, servants, furniture, appliances and even motor cars created to be
burned during funerary rites. Young Chinese girls created paper objects as part
of their bridal trousseaus.

The artistry of the early Chinese craftsman is revealed in many other guises. In
early times, paper money was meticulously hand-cut. Fanciful pin-prick
designs were used from 960 to 1280 A.D. to make perforated tomb paper. The
Chinese papercut, or pierced paper design, is a centuries-old technique. To

U.S. printed design, *Ocean Liner Bremen*, contemporary. Cardboard. Courtesy The Glenbow Museum, Calgary.

*To become paper
is an awesome thing.
Humans, watch closely
these changes.*

MAKOTO OOKE

Mexican papier-mâché figure, twentieth century. 36 x 24 x 8" (91 x 61 x 20 cm).

make a papercut, Chinese artisans used razor-sharp knives along with punches and chisels to cut up to fifty layered papers at a time.

Interest in the Chinese papercut spread, emerging in Persia in the sixteenth century and then in other countries such as Turkey, Holland, Germany, Poland and England. The silhouette portrait is a variation of the papercut and originated in England in 1669. This, along with the diorama, was popularized in the eighteenth century by Queen Anne of England, who amused herself by cutting paper ships arranged in sculptured bas-relief.

The global influence of Chinese papercuts can still be seen today. Present-day Polish cut-paper designs have a rich legacy as religious decorations made to celebrate holidays such as Easter and Christmas. In Mexico, cut-paper designs are used as funerary objects and often feature subjects such as dancing skeletons in humorous scenarios. Cardboard shadow puppets have been crafted with cut-paper techniques by artisans in many countries, notably China, Thailand, Egypt, Greece, Italy and Turkey.

Polish paper cut, twentieth century. Courtesy Maria Muszynski.

Paper has been used to fashion articles for utilitarian, as well as decorative and religious purposes. Among the many utilitarian paper articles produced by Japanese craftsworkers are umbrellas, fans, toys, screens, clothing and other household articles. Of special note is shifu (paper clothing) items, which employ threadlike strips of paper woven on a loom and sewn into kimonos and other articles of clothing.

The largest paper sculptures—still made in Valencia, Spain—are the fallas, which are papier-mâché figures often rising several stories high. These sculptures are designed to be burned in conjunction with the rites of crema, the celebration of the first day of spring and/or the purge of evil.

14

2

Materials,
Tools,
Techniques

Forms made by rolling triangular papers
over dowels.

Every material has unique qualities that entreat the artist to respect and handle it in accord with its nature. Sculptor Henry Moore was sensitive to this notion when he spoke of "truth to materials" and the need for establishing a sympathetic relationship between artists and their materials. True craftsworkers nurture respect for tools and materials and treat them kindly. Through experience, they learn such empathy is necessary to make a product that is integrated in concept, technique and substance. George Nakashima, a master woodworker from New Hope, Pennsylvania, expressed his respect for trees and wood—his art medium—in this way: "We work with boards from those trees, to fulfill their yearning for a second life, to release their richness and beauty. From these planks we fashion objects useful to man, and if nature wills, things of beauty. In any case, these objects harmonize the rhythms of nature to fulfill the tree's destiny and ours."

The noted Bauhaus teacher Josef Albers encouraged his students to experiment freely with materials before embarking on serious endeavors. He admonished young learners to temporarily suspend their notions about making art and simply enjoy discovering congenial ways of handling specific materials. His stu-

**Bas-relief paper sculpture, 20 x 20"
(51 x 51 cm). Author's design workshop,
The University of Calgary.**

16

dents developed respect and sensitivity for their tools and materials as well as realizing that the stages of planning and making are not separate, but interwoven activities. Herein lies an important lesson: Free experimentation—and serendipity—often leads to great discoveries. Exploration gives the artist a vocabulary of technical expression that can be applied to creative effort.

Paper: The Medium

Cellulose is the material that constitutes the chief part of the cell walls of plants. The process of preparing plant fiber to be used for paper—beating, boiling and washing—serves to dissolve lignin, pectin, waxes and gums from the plant material, leaving primarily the cellulose fiber which is required for papermaking. A fortuitous quality of cellulose fibers is that they form a self-adhering, continuous mat when dried from water suspension. Some fibers commonly used to make paper include the following:

The surface of a pure white sheet of paper is sensitive to even a small spot of dirt. If the young craftsman regards his work irreverently, he erases the smile from the face of the beautiful goddess.

SADAMI YAMADA

Abaca, derived from the leaf stems and trunks of a type of banana tree grown in the Philippines. Often referred to as Manila hemp.

Bagasse, a fiber derived from sugar cane.

Bast fiber, any of a number of plant fibers derived from the inner bark of plants. Includes flax, jute, ramie, hemp, kozo, mitsumata and gampi.

Cotton, available in the form of cotton linter, cotton rag and raw cotton.

Esparto, a fiber from the esparto grass plant.

Flax, a bast fiber which is processed to form flax tow, a papermaking fiber.

Gampi, a Japanese inner bark fiber derived from the wikstroemia cannescens plant.

Jute, a glossy fiber of two East Indian plants.

Kapok, a seed-hair fiber from the South Pacific used to make translucent sheets.

Kozo, a common Japanese inner bark fiber derived from the kozo (paper mulberry) plant.

Line flax, a bast fiber. Linen is produced from line flax which has been combed clean of straw.

Maguey, gray-brown in color, derived from a type of agave plant.

Mitsumata, an inner bark fiber used in Oriental papermaking, from the thymelaeceae shrub.

Russian hemp, an unrefined fiber, combed to remove most of the straw.

Silk, a protein fiber produced by caterpillars.

Sisal, derived from a leaf fiber. Has a golden color.

Wheat straw, a grass fiber which has long strands of fiber and a distinctive golden color.

Note: "Rice paper" is a catch-all phrase erroneously used to describe Japanese papers such as kozo or mulberry. Although such papers have a rice-like appearance in their color and transparency, rice has nothing to do with their production. For detailed information regarding fibers for papermaking, consult books listed in the bibliography.

Qualities of Paper

The chief ingredient in most low-grade commercial papers, such as newsprint, is wood cellulose. Finer grades of paper contain a percentage of cotton or are made up of 100 percent cotton rag fiber. Important characteristics of paper include acidity, sizing, finish, grain, weight and sheet size.

Acidity The pH balance of paper—its acid versus alkaline content—is determined by the fibers and other materials used to make the paper. The pH scale ranges from pH 1 (complete acidity) to pH 14 (complete alkalinity). Papers with high acid content eventually darken and become brittle. A good quality art paper is acid free and buffered to a neutral pH, between six and eight.

Sizing Sizing is a substance added during manufacturing to make paper less absorbent and more suitable for painting, drawing, printing and forming. Weak solutions of sizing such as gelatin or hide glue may be mixed with stock in the formation of paper; this is called internal sizing. When sizing is applied to one or both surfaces after paper is made, the process is called surface-sizing. Lithographic and other fine art paper is usually surface-sized to increase surface strength. Some types of papers, however, are available unsized for artists who require an absorbent surface.

Finish Finish denotes the appearance of a paper and the way it feels to the touch. There are three main categories of finish: antique (papers with a soft, vellum or "toothy" finish), machine finish (papers made more compact, smoother or shinier by calendering, i.e. being pressed between a series of steel rollers) and coated (papers made smooth by a coating of fine clay, which is flowed onto the surface with adhesives and compressed with smooth rollers). Many art papers are available in several different finishes. Bristol board, for example, is available in plate (smooth) and vellum (slightly toothy) surfaces. Some papers are subjected to treatments after formation and drying to enhance certain desirable characteristics. Such operations include smoothing, embossing, coating, waxing, laminating, impregnating, corrugating and printing.

Every master knows that the material teaches the artist.

ILYA EHRENBURG, TWENTIETH
CENTURY RUSSIAN WRITER

Other finishes of artists' papers include cold-pressed (CP) and not-pressed (NP), which have an open or coarse texture. Some of the heaviest grades of paper are available in rough, which denotes a paper of even coarser grain. Hot-pressed (HP) are papers that have been pressed between heated metal plates for a smoother, more glossy surface, making them better for opaque, rather than watercolor, decoration. Note that quality papers are identified by the manufacturer's watermark or embossment in a corner; the side of the paper upon which the logo appears denotes the "right," or finished, side of the paper. Deckled describes papers with feathery, untrimmed edges.

Grain Grain refers to the way fibers are aligned within the paper's structure. If the fibers run parallel to the paper's long side, the paper has vertical grain. If the fibers run parallel to its short side, the paper has horizontal grain. In the paper trade, the grain's direction is shown as the second dimension in measurements. For example, a paper that measures 25" x 38" is long-grain because the 38" indicates the direction of the grain. Paper is more easily bent, folded, creased, scored and torn along the grain, than against it. You can determine the grain of light-weight or medium-weight paper by one of two methods: (1) Hold lighterweight paper up to a strong light and observe the alignment, or direction, of the fibers

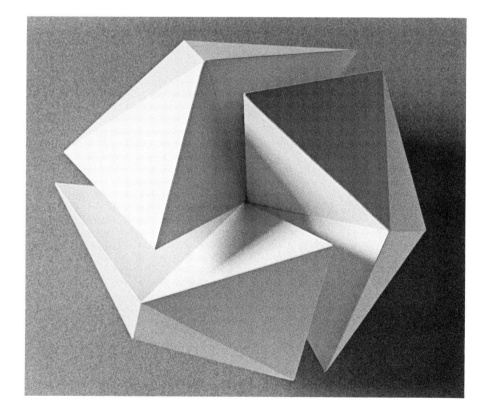

Three-dimensional composition with regular tetrahedrons. Workshop of Franz Zeier, Zurich.

or (2) Moisten a corner of the paper, then rip it in two opposite directions. Ripping is more easily done with the grain than against it. The best way to determine a paper's strength is to crease and fold two sample sheets in opposite directions, stand them up and see which of the two stays most erect without curling or bending.

Weight   A paper's weight refers to how much a ream (500 sheets) weighs in a given size, known as the basis weight. For example, 500 sheets of 17" x 22" bond paper weigh 20 pounds, therefore its basis weight is 20 pounds, and it is called 20 lb. paper. If a paper is said to be 40M, it means that 1000 sheets of its basic size weigh 40 pounds—the basis weight. European-made papers are expressed in grams per one square meter of a particular paper. Thus, a 200g paper indicates that a section measuring 1 meter x 1 meter weighs 200 grams. Thin papers are about 72 pounds, intermediate 90, fairly heavy 140, and heavy-weight 250 to 400 pounds. The latter come in board-like sheets.

Sheet size   There are many standard sheet sizes. Some of the more commonly used papers (such as drawing paper in 40-, 50-, 60- or 80-pound weight) are available in standard sizes of 9 x 12", 12 x 18", 18 x 24" and 24 x 36". Although there are variations from different countries and mills, some of the standard sizes by which fine papers are known internationally are by the following designations and dimensions: royal (19 x 24"), super-royal (19 ½ x 27"), imperial (22 x 30"), elephant (23 x 28"), double elephant (26 ½ x 40") and antiquarian (31 x 53"). Some fine art paper (such as Arches 90- or 140-pound) is available in 44 x 10 yard rolls. Common sizes for text and cover papers manufactured for the printing industry are 23 x 35", 25 x 38" and 26 x 40". The standard sheet size for bond paper is 17 x 22", which provides four standard-size 8 ½ x 11" letterheads per sheet.

Commercially Available Papers

Many types of commercial (machine-made) papers are suitable for collage and paper sculpture. A good paper is simply one that suits the task at hand. To make a three-dimensional sculpture, for example, you might require a paper that is flexible yet strong enough to support its own weight, as well as being adaptable for techniques such as creasing, cutting, bending, folding and rolling. On the other hand, to make a collage, you might want transparent and/or translucent papers. In yet another application, say for making larger artworks, heavy-weight cardboard might be appropriate. Some machine-made papers suitable for paper sculpture include the following:

Light-weight papers

Ingres charcoal paper, 60 lb. (available in a variety of colors)

Cartridge drawing paper, 30–35 lb.

Bristol board drawing paper, 1 ply

Carlyle drawing paper, 65 lb.

Strathmore drawing paper, 60 lb.

Construction paper, medium–lightweight (available in most colors)

Medium-weight papers (ideal for geometric constructions)

Mayfair drawing paper, 80 lb.

Strathmore drawing paper (300 or 400 series), 70 lb., 80 lb.

Mi-Teintes pastel paper, 80 lb. (available in a variety of colors)

Bristol board drawing paper, 2 ply (100 lb.), 3 ply (130 lb.)

Morilla drawing paper, 80 lb.

Fabriano watercolor paper (classico or artistico), 90 lb.

Bockingford watercolor paper, 90 lb.

Arches Velin or BFK printmaking paper, 80 lb.

Carlyle drawing paper, 100 lb.

Arches watercolor paper, 90 lb.

Stonehenge printmaking paper, 120 lb. (available in white, cream, fawn, gray, tan)

Heavier medium-weight papers

Fabriano watercolor paper (classico, artistico or esportazione, a handmade
     paper), 140 lb.

Bockingford watercolor paper, 140 lb.

Arches watercolor paper, 140 lb.

Alexis watercolor paper, 140 lb.

Waterford watercolor paper, 140 lb.

Heavy-weight papers and boards

Whatman watercolor paper, 140 lb., 200 lb.

Waterford watercolor paper, 250 lb.

Bockingford watercolor paper, 250 lb.

Arches watercolor paper, 300 lb., 400 lb.

Bristol board, 4 ply, 5 ply

Stag blank, 6 ply (also available in heavier plys)

Railroad board, 4 ply, 6 ply (available in white and assorted colors)

Showcard (poster) board (Crescent, Bainbridge or Peterboro)

Fabriano watercolor paper, 300 lb.

Corrugated paper (in white, brown and assorted colors)

John Babcock, *Eye of the Storm,* 1990. Cast handmade paper, 32 x 60 x 3" (61 x 152 x 8 cm). Courtesy the artist.

Specialty papers

Metallic paper, a paper-backed metal foil (available in gold, silver and assorted colors)

Origami paper, a lightweight paper, colored on one side (available in assorted colors)

Fluorescent-colored paper (available in assorted weights and non-lightfast colors)

Silhouette paper, a lightweight paper with a smooth black face

Duet art paper, a lightweight paper, each side is a different color

Aluminum foil (available in rolls of silver and assorted colors)

Transparent cellophane (available in sheets of assorted colors)

Tissue paper (available in sheets of assorted colors)

Velour paper, covered on one side with a velvet-like surface (available in assorted colors)

Fome Core board, a brand name for a lightweight, plastic board, faced on both sides with white paper (available in several sizes and thicknesses)

Japanese papers (hosho, inomachi, kochi, kozo, muchizuki, torinoka)

Custom-Made Papers

Independent paper mills make limited quantities of handmade, decorative and specialty papers suitable for collage, cut-paper and other sculptural applications. These include decorative Japanese lace papers, papers with metallic or other embedded materials, and papers with built-in color or other optical qualities. Although they are not generally available from art stores, they can be obtained directly from suppliers by mail order. (See Sources of Supplies, page 149.)

Handmade Paper

At some point in your studio experiments, you will want to make your own paper from ready-to-use pulp. This material can be reconstituted with an ordinary kitchen blender, an electric drill outfitted with a paint stirrer, or with machines known as hydropulpers. Pulp can be used for modeling and casting, for making collages and assemblages, or for creating mixed media artworks and three-dimensional paintings. It may be purchased either in wet form (supplied in gallon pails) or as dry sheets such as Abaca or cotton linters.

Getting Started: Tools and Materials

To make paper sculpture with the commercially available papers described in this chapter you will need the following:

- *Work surface:* sheet of pulp board, which is an inexpensive, high-density cardboard, to protect table surfaces.
- *Tools for measuring and designing:* ruler, triangle, compass, right angle, protractor, pencil, eraser, dividers.
- *Tools for ruling and cutting:* ruler, steel edge, triangle, compasses, pencil, eraser, dividers, scissors, mat or utility knife, X-acto knife.

Basic tools for making paper sculpture: ruler, stencil knife, mat knife, scissors, creaser, dividers, compass, pencil, eraser, right angle, protractor, cellulose tape, glue stick, staplers.

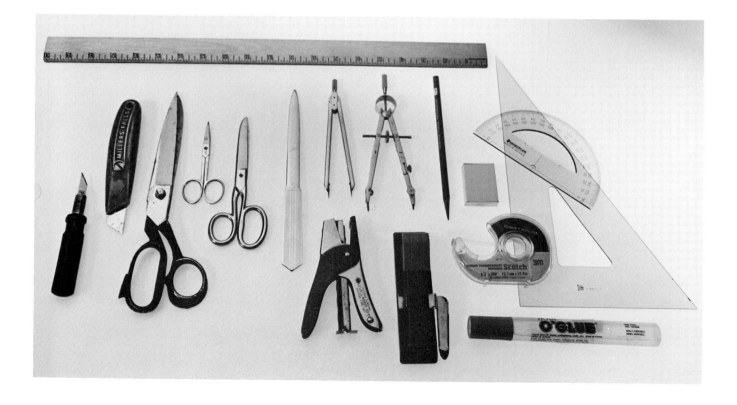

23

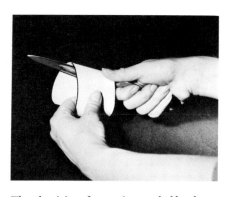

The plasticity of paper is revealed by the way it assumes and holds new forms. Here, a flat sheet of paper is curled by being drawn over the edge of a letter opener.

- *Tools for creasing, scoring, folding and rolling:* blunt kitchen knife or letter opener, mat knife, ruler, right angle, dowels and other cylindrical forms.
- *Tools for joining and fastening:* stapler, paper clips, cellophane tape, double-face tape, glue.
- *Studio illumination:* Daylight illumination is preferred. Avoid fluorescent bulbs, which produce flat lighting; instead, use incandescent light, preferably a flexible-arm lamp in conjunction with a ceiling light.
- *Other useful accessories:* guillotine paper cutter, French curves, circle cutter, tweezers, fine wire, needle and thread, pins, tacks.

The sculptor's quest is to transform a flat sheet of paper or pulp into a three-dimensional form in accordance with an idea or inspiration. An innate quality of paper is its plasticity; it can be shaped into a three-dimensional form and will maintain that form, rather than springing back to its original, flat shape. Some basic ways of exploring paper—and its plasticity—are by:

- cutting
- creasing/scoring/folding
- curling
- tearing
- piercing
- weaving
- winding

- wrinkling/crumpling
- layering
- joining
- modeling
- casting
- decorating
- combining with other media

Safety

Although paper may not be considered a dangerous working material, there are hazards associated with creating sculpture in paper, and general safety precautions should be heeded whenever possible. This is especially true when using sharp tools, motorized machinery and materials that involve solvents or other noxious fumes. Use common sense in the art studio; establish safety guidelines and procedures to ensure proper handling of all materials and tools. Prepare your work space to accommodate the task at hand; this includes insuring that there is adequate ventilation at all times and providing protective garments such as aprons, safety goggles and gloves, if necessary. While safety notes appear repeatedly throughout this book, it is incumbent upon you to take adequate precautions regarding safe and proper conduct in the art studio.

For additional information on safety, refer to *Safety in the Artroom,* by Charles A. Qualley (Davis Publications, Inc., 1986).

Techniques and Explorations

Cutting

With Scissors Good quality scissors are essential for making clean cuts. In order to produce effective cut-paper shapes, short, choppy strokes should be avoided. Smooth, continuous cuts are easily obtained by holding the scissors steady in one hand while feeding the paper; the scissor blades should be opened, then slowly closed as the paper is fed. Manicure scissors are useful for making small or more delicate cuts. Pinking shears are useful for decorative zig-zag cuts.

With the Knife A sharp mat knife and a metal straightedge are essential tools for making straight cuts. The table should be protected with a sheet of pulp board, which is used as a work surface. An X-acto knife may be employed for cutting curved and more complicated shapes. Always use more than one stroke to cut through heavy-weight papers. The guillotine cutter is useful for cutting a large number of strips or shapes.

> *Safety Note:* Keep fingers well back on the straightedge while using a knife.

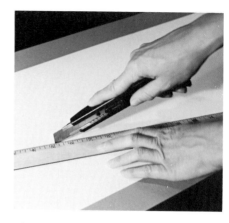

The mat knife and ruler are used to make straight cuts.

Clean-cut edges are produced by moving the paper into the scissors while cutting.

Paper takes on a spatial quality when it is folded or bent along creased or scored lines.

Creasing, Scoring, Folding

Creasing is done by drawing a blunt tool such as a letter opener over the paper surface, leaving an indentation in preparation for making a cleanly folded edge. Aside from a letter opener, other good creasers include a dull kitchen knife, a bone folder, a wooden modeling tool and a key. Note that creasing produces a raised line on the other side of the paper. When the paper is folded, the line should be on the inside of the fold. Scoring is similar to creasing, except that instead of a blunt tool, a sharp knife is used to partially cut the paper surface. Thicker papers and cardboard are scored rather than creased. The techniques of creasing or scoring in conjunction with folding impart structural strength to paper and allow it to become a self-supporting material.

Curling

Curling is a way of transforming paper into curved shapes and forms. Narrow strips can be curled by simply pressing them down with the flat side of a knife and pulling them over the edge of the blade. Larger sheets can be drawn over the edge of a table or under a ruler, which makes them pop into curved forms. Paper can also be curled by being rolled with the grain over dowels, knitting needles or other cylindrical forms.

Three-dimensional shapes produced by curling.

Pierced paper rolled to form a cylinder. A nail, knife and Phillips screwdriver were the only tools used to produce the textured surface.

Tearing

Tearing produces a ragged edge, in sharp contrast to the clean edge made by cutting. No tools other than hands are required for achieving this distinctive deckle edge. Torn shapes can be further enhanced by curling, creasing, bending, joining, decorating, etc.

Piercing

Piercing—poking holes through paper—is a delightful way of creating textures and designs. You can achieve a variety of surface effects by repeatedly puncturing paper with commonplace tools such as sharpened sticks, nails, hole punches, screwdrivers or sewing or knitting needles. Paper should be pierced over a soft surface such as a carpet remnant. The braille-like texture is revealed on the paper's reverse side.

> *Safety Note:* Use care with sharp instruments. Always point sharp tools away from your body and keep hands well away from direct piercing action.

Weaving

There are many ways to weave sculptural forms out of paper. One is by interlacing paper strips, weaving them into a paper matrix. Another is by interlacing paper strips into objects that have slotted or gridded shapes, such as perforated boxes, baskets, window blinds or other found objects. Conventional floor looms can also be employed using a linen warp, or length-wise threads, and paper strips as weft, or cross-wise fibers.

Distinctive deckle edges produced by tearing paper.

Paper can be interlaced in many ways and with mixed materials to form unusual relief or basket-like forms. Here, puckering and manipulation of paper strips turn a simple paper weaving into a dynamic sculptural form.

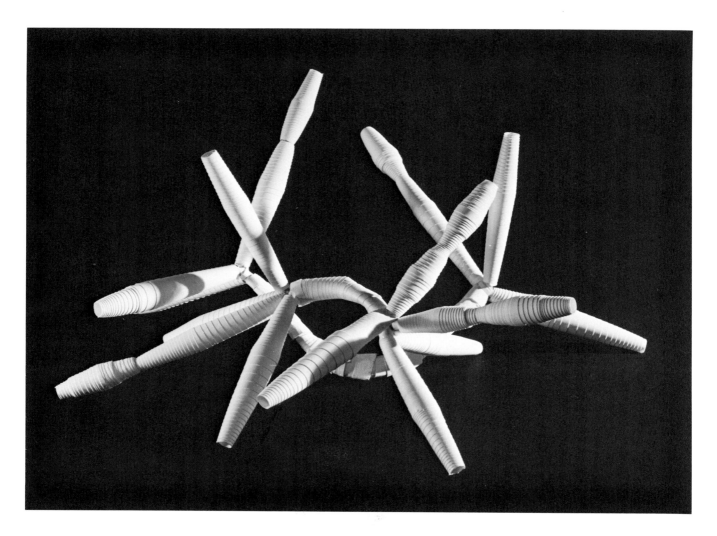

Modular beads made by winding triangular papers tightly over dowels or other cylindrical objects. Beads can be attached to form a wearable necklace or, as here, to create a freestanding sculpture.

Winding

Distinctive sculptural forms can be created by winding strips of paper around skeletal structures made of wood, metal, wire, rope or other linear material. The wound paper adds volume to the underlying structure and can be further enhanced by painting. To make paper beads, roll elongated, triangular paper strips tightly over a wood dowel or knitting needle. Glue the strips' ends, then slide them off the dowel or needle used to shape them. Spiral forms are produced by rolling papers cut into 45-degree triangles tightly over a tubular mold. When released from the mold, they hold the spiral shape.

Wrinkling/Crumpling

Paper that has been folded, crushed or wrinkled and then unfolded and laid flat again—either by deliberate or serendipitous means—will yield interesting surface patterns and textures. The effects can provide dramatic contrast to the pristine quality of untextured areas in terms of surface and tonal variations.

Tissue and other types of flexible papers were folded and/or crumpled, then pressed flat and glued to a background to create this textured surface.

Layering

In this process, cardboard or paper shapes are overlaid on a ground plane. Depending on the thickness of the materials and number of layers used, the overlaid shapes can yield a surface that is either flat, as in a collage, or three-dimensional, as in a bas-relief or a three-dimensional topographical map.

Joining

Both flat and three-dimensional shapes of paper may be adhered to a background panel with white glue or other quick-set adhesives. Found objects for use in mixed media techniques may require the use of silicone adhesive or five-minute epoxy.

By Gluing Glues should be selected according to the type of paper used and the task at hand. Do not use library paste, cellulose glue or rubber cement; these materials quickly lose their adhesive properties. White glue is an excellent choice, but use it sparingly; too much will produce unsightly marks and cause lightweight paper to pucker or warp. If necessary, use paper clips to hold parts

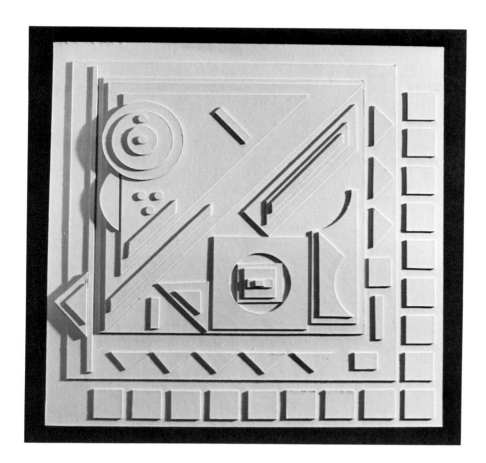

Bas-relief created by overlaying cardboard shapes.

together while glue sets. Glue sticks are easy to use but do not give lasting results. A thick adhesive such as silicone seal or five-minute epoxy is a good choice for attaching three-dimensional paper forms and found objects to each other or to flat materials.

> *Safety Note:* Heed manufacturer's warnings and safety precautions while using glues.

By Notching Notching provides an easy way to join shapes of medium- or heavy-weight paper. Short slots are made on each of the shapes to be joined so they can slip together perpendicularly. To join two shapes using this technique, make two parallel cuts on each shape with a mat or utility knife. To make a slot, cut away the paper between the two cuts. Make sure the width of the slot on each shape is exactly the same as the thickness of the adjoining paper. The notched shapes can then be interlocked to form larger structures and configurations. Note that the length of each slot will determine how deeply the shapes will interlock. A related way of joining paper without gluing is by employing a system of slits and tabs (see page 77 for more details on creating tabs).

Safety Note: Be sure to keep fingers away from the cutting edge when using a utility knife. For best results, use a knife with a sharp blade and make several light scoring marks rather than a single, deep cut.

Alternate Ways Besides glues and adhesives, other products used to join paper include tape, string, thread, wire, clips, fasteners and staples.

Modeling with Papier-Mâché

The traditional papier-mâché technique—the layer method—calls for torn pieces of paper to be dipped into an adhesive and applied to a form or mold. By overlapping up to ten layers of paper, a thick shell is produced that can be removed from the form and painted or decorated. Papier-mâché can also be applied over armatures that are allowed to remain within the finished product as a substructure. Commercially made papier-mâché paste, white glue and acrylic polymer medium are recommended adhesives for making papier-mâché laminates.

Shapes can be joined by using tabs and slits, or by notching and interlocking.

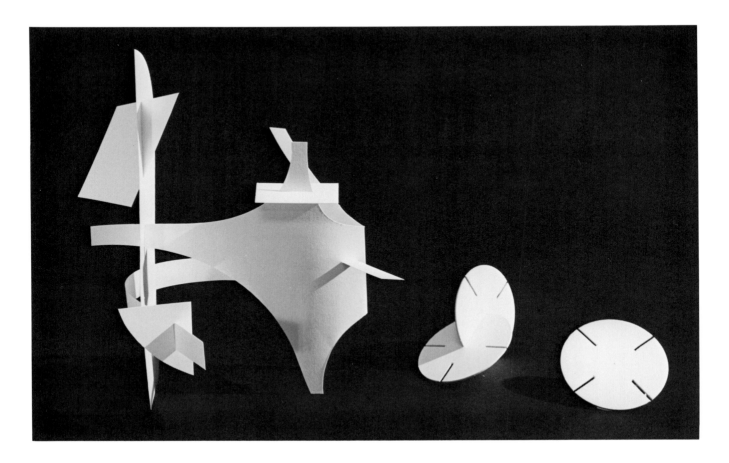

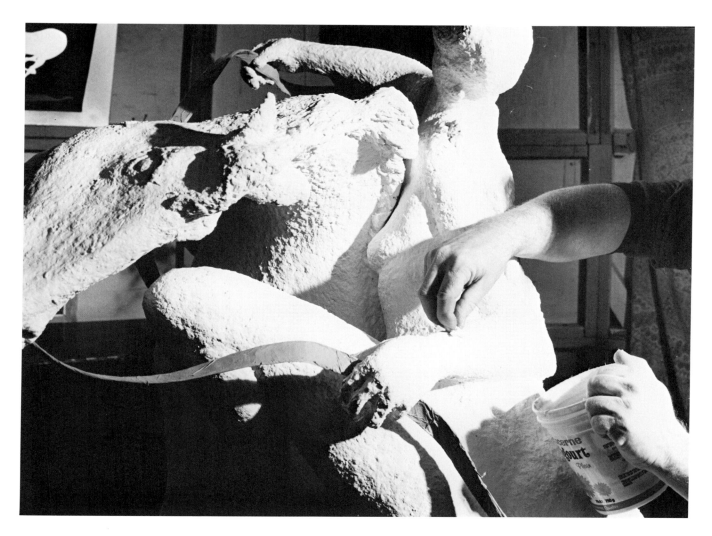

The pulp method offers another way of using papier-mâché. Here, paper pulp is often mixed with white glue in a cottage cheese-like consistency. The material can be used like modeling clay and is an excellent medium for making three-dimensional artworks. In another variation of the pulp method, facial tissue can be dipped in an adhesive mixture, compressed to form a "modeling clay" and used to fashion sculptural features or objects.

Papier-mâché (pulp method) is used over a wire armature to create a sculptural form. Courtesy Peter Smith.

Casting with Pulp

In hand papermaking, cellulose fiber is beaten into pulp, mixed with water to make a soupy substance known as slurry, and scooped out of the water so that the fibers interlock to form a strong bond. With the use of a frame system known as a mold and deckle, this pulp is easily formed into sheets, which, while

Karen Trask, *Le Poids des Mots, Between Hands,* 1989. Cast in paper from molds made from the artist's hands and torso. Courtesy the artist.

Arndt von Diepenbroick, *Lily,* 1988. Papier-mâché (layer method) over wire, 67 x 18 x 20" (1.74 x .45 x .55 m). Courtesy the artist.

still wet, can be cast in molds, layered over structures or used in collage, assemblage and other applications. Fiber is available from independent papermakers in the form of wet, ready-to-use pulp or as dry sheets. The dry pulp is easily rehydrated with a kitchen blender or a hydropulper.

Decorating

Among the many ways of decorating paper with color are brushing, spattering, sponging, printing, airbrushing, rolling with paint rollers and marbling. You may also paint with watercolors, inks, dyes, oil paints, acrylics, enamels or metallic and antique coatings, or embellish surfaces with pencil drawing, designs in chalk, pastels, colored pencils, pen and ink or crayons. Other decorations include wax resist, printing, calligraphy, collage and assemblage. Loose materials such as sand, glitter, sequins, ribbons and leathers can be applied either to the paper's surface or between laminae. Designs and patterns can be painted on surfaces either before or after paper has been shaped into three-dimensional forms.

The bas-relief design, created by overlaying flat shapes, is further enriched with sprayed and spattered color. Edgar Buonagurio, *Premonition,* 1988. Museum board, 22 x 19" (56 x 48 cm). Courtesy the artist.

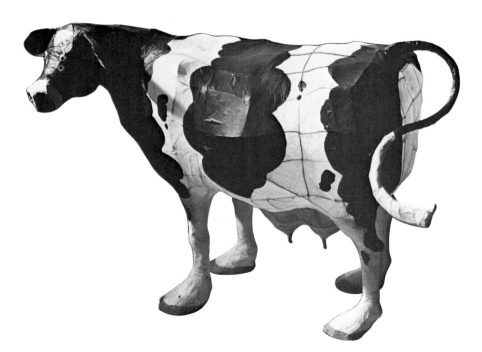

Frances Semple, *Cow,* 1990. Tissue over
wire armature, 22 x 18 x 6" (56 x 46 x 15 cm).
Courtesy the artist.

Maggie Tchir, *Mountain Memory Box/
Dance of the Northern Lights,* 1990.
Handmade paper, mixed media, 12 x 12 x
14" (30 x 30 x 35 cm). Courtesy the artist.

Mixed Media

There is virtually no limit to how paper can be combined with other materials. Experimentally minded artists have produced artworks that combine paper with wood, metal, stone, ceramic, bone, fiber, feathers, plastic, glass, gravel, sand, machine parts and found objects. An unusual way of using paper and mixed media is to apply thin paper such as wrapping tissues or handmade Japanese papers over skeletal structures made of wood, bamboo, reed, wire or metal—a technique that yields attractive translucent surfaces. Making collages, assemblages, artists' books or other mixed media artworks offers opportunities to combine paper with virtually any material.

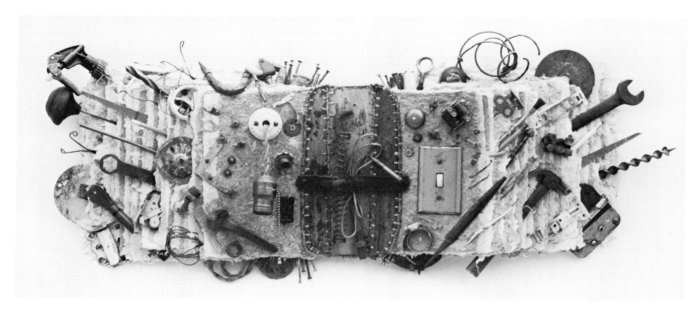

Colleen Barry, *Tool Book.* Handmade paper and mixed media, 13 x 34 x 4" (33 x 86 x 10 cm). Courtesy the artist.

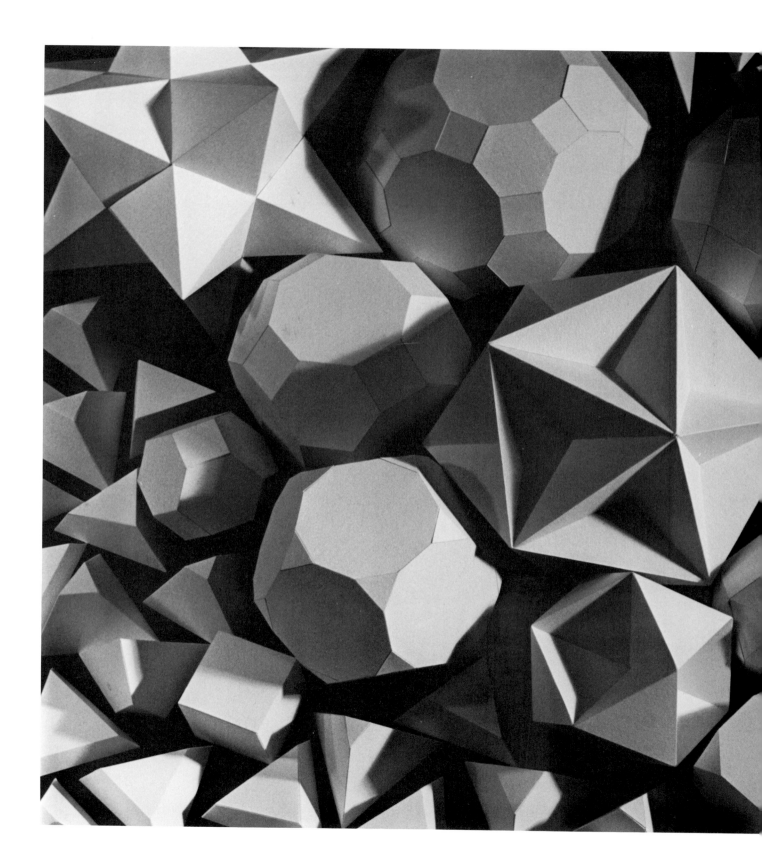

3

Basic Shapes and Forms

Dimensional forms.

The Creation of Three-Dimensional Form

The reason we perceive certain objects as being three-dimensional is that they present different "pictures" when viewed from different angles. This perception is in contrast to that of two-dimensional drawings and paintings, which offer only single, fixed viewpoints regardless of the viewer's position. Every three-dimensional form has, in essence, kinetic properties—qualities of being in motion. Although a sculpture itself may not be kinetic or changing, the visual response to it is. Therefore, sculpture is a product that involves time—the fourth dimension. In this regard, the anonymous sage who observed that "Every sculpture comprises a thousand drawings" was absolutely correct.

The discerning teachers at the Bauhaus school of design in Germany referred to three-dimensional art as "space modulators." They focused attention on the fact that a sculpture is essentially an object that interplays form and space, positive and negative volumes and the tonalities of light that strike its surface. Notice, for example, that when a sheet of paper is folded and set on end, it not only becomes three-dimensional, but also an object that reflects light in complex patterns.

We can summarize that every three-dimensional construction is, in essence, a kinetic object, a space modulator and a light reflector. This is not to overlook, of course, that a sculpture—above all—is an object that reveals the explorations and sentiments of the artist.

The combination and interaction of planes is the essence of sculpture. Like other art forms, sculpture evolves from the manipulation of some of the basic elements of design: line, plane, texture, tone, color and volume. In sculpture, however, these elements are not illusionary, as they are in painting, but three-dimensional. A sculptural line is an edge that separates adjoining spatial planes. Adjoining planes, in turn, produce volumetric form. Edges, planes and volumes are integrated to produce sculptural form.

Some basic planes, three-dimensional forms and variations—along with patterns to construct them—are presented in the pages that follow.

We live, in fact, in a three-dimensional world. What we see in front of us is not a flat picture with length and breadth only, but an expanse with physical depth—the third dimension.

WUCIOUS WONG, TEACHER
AND AUTHOR

Three-dimensional paper forms. From the workshop of Bob Stowell, The University of Calgary.

43

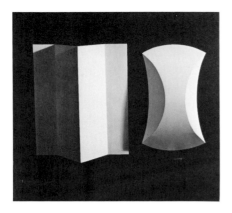

Rectilinear and curvilinear planes are produced by creasing and folding paper in straight or curved lines.

Basic Planes and Three-Dimensional Forms

When a piece of paper is creased by a straight line and then folded, two rectilinear planes are produced. When paper is creased with a curved line, curvilinear planes are produced. Sculpture is composed of rectilinear planes, curvilinear planes, combined rectilinear/curvilinear planes, cones, cylinders, polyhedra, pyramids, prisms and cubes.

Standard cylinders are composed of two identical circles that are parallel to each other and attached by a perpendicular tube.

Prisms have identical ends and parallel sides. A basic prism has square ends, while other prisms can have triangular, polygonal or irregularly shaped ends.

The standard cone has a circular base, a vertex (highest point directly above the center of the base) and a surface made by connecting every point on the outside edge of the base to the vertex.

The standard pyramid has a square base with four triangular walls that meet at the vertex.

Basic forms (from left): cylinder, hexagonal prism, triangular prism, cone and pyramid. Courtesy Bob Stowell.

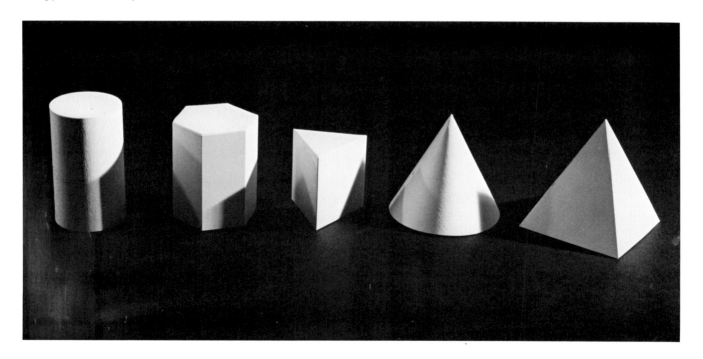

44

1

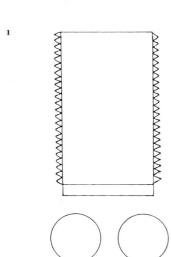

2

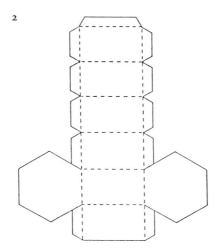

3

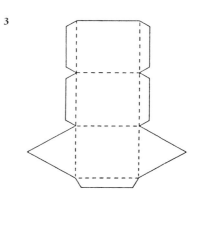

4

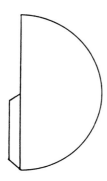

5

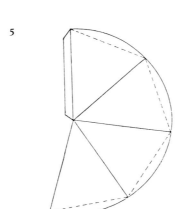

Patterns for constructing basic forms.
1) Cylinder, 2) hexagonal prism,
3) triangular prism, 4) cone, 5) pyramid.

45

The truncated icosahedron has twenty faces and twenty vertices. Other geometric solids can also be modified by truncation, or slicing off the corners.

A polygon is a two-dimensional plane surface formed by the end to end connection of straight lines. A polyhedron is a three-dimensional form made up of connected polygons. The planes of the polygons join together to make a closed volumetric form such that each side of every polygon is shared with the side of another. The sides of the polygons intersect at their ends to form vertices, the points where lines meet. Therefore, polygons are the faces of a polyhedron. A polyhedron is categorized as regular if all its faces are identical and equal polygons and all of its vertices are alike.

The stellated dodecahedron can be created by attaching a five-sided pyramid to each of the dodecahedron's twelve faces.

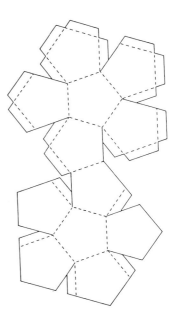

Pattern for constructing a dodecahedron.

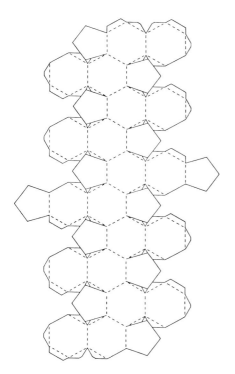

Pattern for constructing the truncated icosahedron.

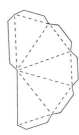

Pattern for constructing a five-sided pyramid.

1

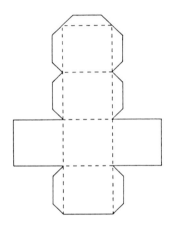

2

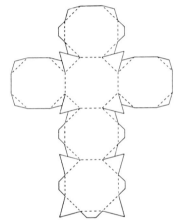

An evolution of forms: The hexahedron (cube, left) progresses to the truncated hexahedron (cube with corners sliced off), to the cuboctahedron (fourteen faces), to the truncated octahedron (fourteen faces, twenty-four vertices or outstanding points, thirty-six edges), to the octahedron (eight faces).

Patterns for constructing 1) hexahedron, 2) truncated hexahedron, 3) cuboctahedron, 4) truncated octahedron, 5) octahedron.

3

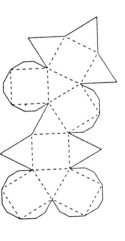

4

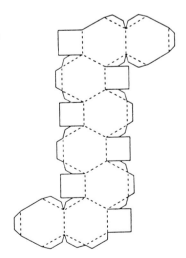

5

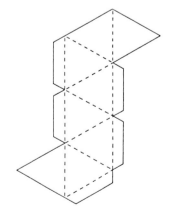

The five Platonic solids (from left): tetrahedron, hexahedron (or cube), octahedron, dodecahedron and icosahedron. Each form possesses planar facets of exactly the same shape.

1

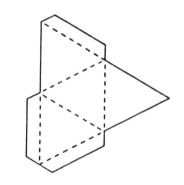

2

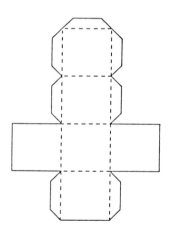

Patterns for constructing the Platonic solids: 1) tetrahedron, 2) hexahedron, 3) octahedron, 4) dodecahedron, 5) icosahedron. Cut on the solid lines. Crease and fold on dotted lines; apply glue to tabs prior to assembly.

Plato was apparently the first person to develop a classification of basic geometric shapes. The five Platonic solids—the tetrahedron, octahedron, hexahedron, icosahedron and dodecahedron—are regular polyhedra which are bounded by identical polygonal faces in which all vertices are equivalent.

Using Patterns to Construct Three-Dimensional Forms

An easy way to create geometric forms with the patterns in this book is to enlarge them on a photocopier to the desired size. The patterns can be transferred onto medium-weight paper (such as Mayfair) by tracing with carbon paper or a graphite sheet. The solid lines on the patterns indicate the outside edges of the shapes, and are guidelines for cutting out the shapes. The dotted lines indicate edges of polygons, and should be used as guidelines for creasing and folding. The patterns also include tabs for gluing and holding the forms together.

3

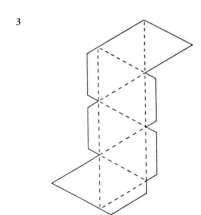

4

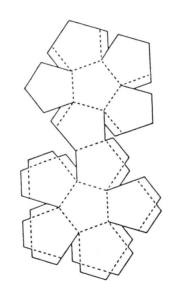

5

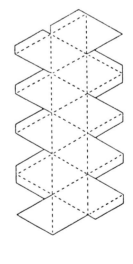

Use a ruler or straightedge and an X-acto knife to cut out the geometric shape along the solid lines. Crease along the dotted lines, using a ruler and a creasing instrument such as a letter opener. Next, fold along the creased lines and bend the paper to produce the three-dimensional form. To ensure a pristine surface, make the creased lines over the carbon tracings. Fold the paper inward so that all of the marked guidelines occur on the inside of the constructed form. Use a tiny amount of white glue on each of the tabs, tuck them under the appropriate planes and hold in place for a moment until the glue sets.

Interesting variations of the hexahedron are made possible by creating open cubes. George Vassler, *Variations of the Cube,* 1990. Paper. Courtesy the artist.

Six notched rectangles are interlocked and stacked between flat squares to form a dimensional grid. George Vassler, *The Honeycomb Cube,* 1990. Cardboard. Courtesy the artist.

Patterns for constructing *The Honeycomb Cube.*

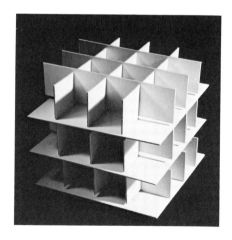

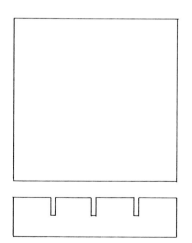

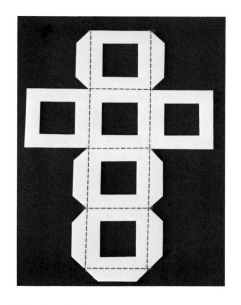  

 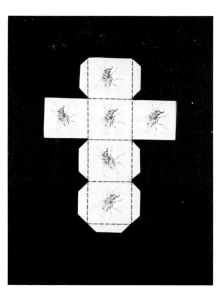

Patterns for _Variations of the Cube._

The constructions you make can be used in many ways—singly, grouped together or with other selected objects in accordance with an idea or concept.

The geometric constructions may be painted, decorated or embellished. Prior to assembly, the patterns may be modified further by cutting to produce skeletal or open volumes for particular design applications.

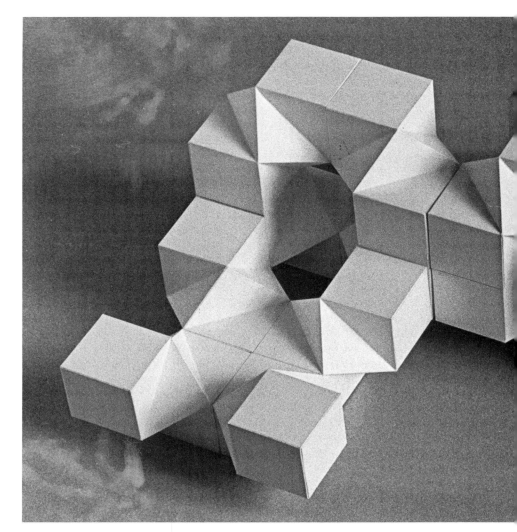

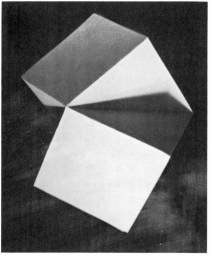

The architectural structure at right was created by repeating the above basic module, the penetrated cube. This module appears to be two interlocking cubes, but it is made from a single sheet of paper using the pattern shown at far right. Franz Zeier, *Modular Construction (with the Penetrated Cube)*, 1974. Paper. Courtesy the artist.

Large-Scale Polyhedra

Make a transparent photocopy of a selected pattern using overhead transparency film designed especially for the photocopier. Place the transparency on an overhead projector, carefully focus and project the enlarged image onto a sheet of heavy-weight cardboard (such as illustration board) which has been taped to a wall. Make sure the cardboard is securely taped to the wall. Carefully trace the enlargement with a sharp pencil and ruler. Place the enlargement on a table protected with chipboard and cut the pattern on the solid lines with a ruler and utility knife.

> *Safety Note:* Make more than one stroke with the knife for each cut and exercise caution to cut **away** from your body.

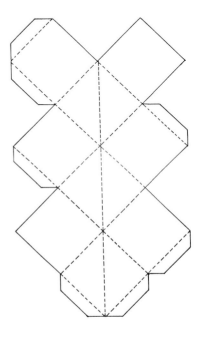

Next, use a straightedge and utility knife to score the cardboard on the dotted lines. Cut halfway into the cardboard, rather than creasing along the dotted lines. Cut off the tabs. Finally, bend the cardboard inward along the score lines to produce the volumetric form. Glue the edges together with white glue. Use masking tape to temporarily hold the shapes together until the glue sets.

Pattern for constructing the penetrated cube.

4
Studio
Experiments

Bruce Beasely, *Construction for Stainless Steel.* Cardboard. Courtesy the artist.

This chapter presents a variety of studio experiments designed to help you explore the potential of paper as a collage and sculpture medium. The information should be regarded as a guide to help you organize and direct your own studio activities. It can easily be modified to suit particular classrooms or individuals. Hopefully, the ideas and exercises will kick-start your imagination as you roll up your sleeves and prepare to engage in a hands-on activity.

Every successful artist realizes that without experimentation there is no advance. Only through personal involvement can we truly know a material, medium or technique that may act as a vehicle for creative expression. Only through trial and error can we discover new hypotheses or variations. As innovator Charles Caleb Colten observed, "Where we cannot invent, we may at least improve; we may give somewhat of novelty to that which was old, condensation to that which was obscure and currency to that which was heretofore concealed." Each of the activities presented in the following pages explores a particular facet of paper sculpture. Together, the activities may serve as a curriculum of study.

Flat shapes are arranged to produce an open spatial structure. Elisabeth Sinken, *Objects 18,* 1989. Cardboard. Courtesy the artist.

They begin with paper cuts and progress through collage, surface treatments, bas-relief, in-the-round constructions, papier-mâché, pulp casting and mixed media. You are encouraged to experiment with different types of papers and techniques and, of course, to imbue them with imagination and invention!

Paper Cuts

The contemporary artist can find wonderful inspirations in the paper cuts made by artisans from China, Japan, Mexico, Holland, Poland and other countries with a legacy of paperwork in folk art. The careful study of such work provides valuable insight into the special techniques that use knives and scissors to produce these fascinating artworks.

Along with either an X-acto knife or scissors, the only materials necessary to make a paper cut are papers such as origami paper (which is colored on one side), typing paper, colored construction paper or any thin, strong paper. For simplicity, paper-cut experiments are classified here in two basic groups: those produced with scissors and folded sheets, and those produced with the knife and flat, unfolded paper.

Strips of handmade paper were colored, woven and overlaid. Parts were stitched together on a sewing machine. Alan Shields, *Long John Barnacle*, 1988. Paper, watercolors, thread, 18 x 52 x 1¾" (46 x 132 x 4.5 cm). Courtesy Paula Cooper Gallery, New York. Photo by Geoffrey Clements.

Ni Fen Kao, *The Fox Pretending to be a Tiger.* Papercut. Courtesy Florence Temko.

Left: Symmetrical papercut. Contemporary Chinese. Courtesy Eddie Lui.

Sister Aloyza, *Decorative Birds.* Papercut. Courtesy Maria Muszynski.

Symmetrical papercut design made with scissors and folded paper. The paper is folded three times (as indicated by the dotted lines) prior to cutting.

Using Scissors and Folded Paper

Both symmetrical and nonsymmetrical paper-cut designs can be produced by this fold-and-cut method. Fold paper in half and cut with scissors to produce a bisymmetrical design. Explore the technique further by folding paper three or four times prior to cutting. Also, discover additional design possibilities by using paper in the shape of a square, rectangle, circle or free form. To make non-symmetrical designs, fold the paper randomly rather than in exact halves, quarters or eighths before cutting.

> *Tip:* Use sharp scissors to cut the paper and move the hand holding the paper into the scissors for a continuous, rather than a choppy, cut.

Using a Knife and Flat Sheets

Start this exercise by making a drawing of a selected motif. Pencil the design on a sheet of white paper that has been cut to exactly the same size as a sheet of origami or other colored paper. Your drawing must be stylized in a manner reminiscent of stained glass design; i.e., the lines, like the leading in stained glass, should be thick, because two cuts will be required to define each line in the paper cut. Additional lines should also be added as required to connect parts that would otherwise fall apart when the design is cut. To establish a visually interesting

60

composition, pay particular attention to the balance between the positive and negative shapes. Place the drawing over the colored paper and tape the superimposed papers to a sheet of pulp board (used as a work surface) in preparation for cutting. Use an X-acto knife to make cuts on both edges of the thick lines. Apply just enough pressure to cut through both papers with a single stroke.

> *Safety Note:* Follow proper procedures and precautions for using knives. Always use sharp blades to decrease the chances of incurring injury.

Finally, remove the white paper that served as a guide to reveal the finished papercut. The completed work may be mounted on paper of contrasting color, glass or a three-dimensional form.

Collage

Collage is sometimes defined as the scissors-and-paste method of adhering paper and miscellaneous materials to a panel. Although it began as a nineteenth century folk art (originally dubbed *papier collé*), the collage was adopted by Cubist, Dadaist and Surrealist artists in the beginning of the twentieth century and elevated from the genre of craft to fine art. Today, artists have expanded the concept of collage to include assemblage and mixed media, wherein three-dimensional objects are also attached to the surface.

You may paint with whatever materials you please: with postage stamps, postcards, playing cards or painted paper.
APOLLINAIRE, FRENCH POET
(1880–1918)

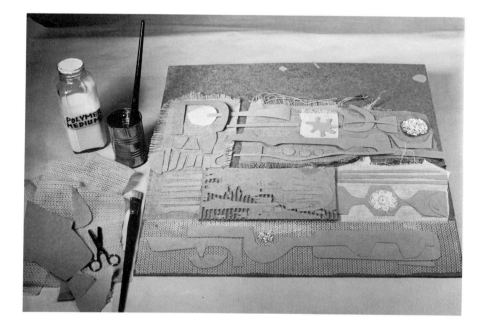

Papers, tissues, cardboard, miscellaneous materials and a proper adhesive are the basic necessities for making collages and assemblages.

To create a collage-in-the-round, papers may be adhered to a sculpture of plaster, papier-mâché, cardboard, clay or wood. William Friesen, *Torso (Collage-in-the-Round)*, 1971. Paper, fired clay, 18 x 6 x 4" (46 x 15 x 10 cm). Courtesy the artist.

Low-Relief Collage

For this experiment, collect various papers such as wallpaper, wrapping paper, tissue, art papers, handmade papers, posters, playing cards, decorative paper bags and placemats, pages from magazines and newspapers, fabrics and cardboard. Cut or tear shapes as desired, and adhere to a panel. Cutting papers with a knife or scissors produces a mechanically clean edge while irregular, or deckled-edge shapes are created by tearing the paper.

Ideal adhesives for gluing papers are white glue and acrylic polymer medium. Glue sticks can also be used, but only where permanence is not necessary. Five-minute epoxy glue or silicone seal are excellent cements for bonding three-dimensional objects to other objects or materials.

Depending on the number of layers applied and their thicknesses, papers that are overlaid on a panel tend to produce a low-relief effect. The three-dimensional effect can be heightened by "collaging" separate pieces of thick cardboard, wood, Fome Core or other objects before adhering them to the base.

Texture

A sheet of heavy-weight rag paper can be easily textured with makeshift tools such as blunted chisels and nails, leather stamping tools and punches, knives

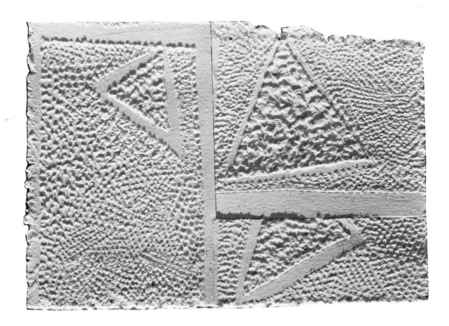

Vito Capone, *Carte*, 1983/84. Sculpted paper. Courtesy the artist.

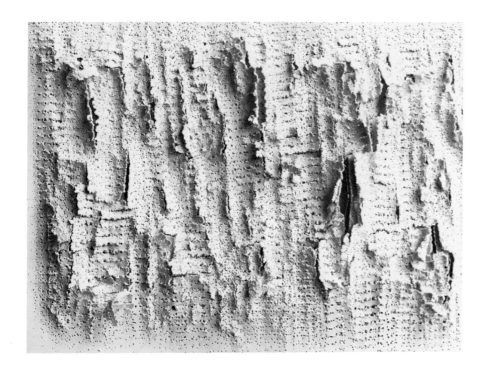

Several layered sheets of paper were textured by piercing. Gerda Klein, *Enriched Surface.* Paper. Courtesy Elisabeth Sinken.

and needles. By manipulating such implements, you can emboss, pierce or engrave the paper. Stamped, or embossed, designs are produced by placing a sheet of paper over a pulp board and striking the hand tools with a mallet. Pierced textures are created by placing a sheet of medium-weight paper over a piece of soft, thick fabric or a rug remnant and puncturing the paper with the sharp implements. Engraved designs are made by dragging the sharp tools over the paper's surface. The textured designs created with each of these techniques will appear in relief on the reverse side of the paper.

Experiment 4
Stamping

Collect a variety of makeshift stamping tools such as blunted nails and chisels, leather stamps and metal tubes, along with a few sheets of medium-weight rag paper and a mallet. You'll also need a sheet of pulp board as a work surface. Start with some preliminary experiments to become familiar with the tools and technique. Divide the paper into a chart with six or nine sections, and tap on the stamping tools with the mallet to create a different embossed texture in each space. Select one or two of the more interesting textures and repeat them on a separate sheet of paper to create an abstract or figurative pattern. Exercise care not to puncture the paper. Produce different effects by varying the intensity of the mallet blow and the angle of the stamping tool. These beginning experi-

Sculptor Vito Capone uses only the stencil knife to engrave textured patterns on the surface of heavy-weight paper.

Pierced paper surfaces can be dramatically textured and patterned.

ments can be developed and expanded upon to create artworks of great interest and complexity.

Piercing

Assemble some sharp-edged and pointed tools, such as sewing needles, sharp nails, knitting needles, knives, Phillip's screwdrivers and chisels, which can be used to puncture a paper's surface. Make an outline drawing in pencil on the working side of a sheet of medium-weight paper. Place the paper over a soft, thick cloth or a smooth-surfaced carpet remnant. Then, texture the paper by making repetitive punctures with selected tools. Remember, the reverse side of the paper will be the finished side of your design.

Engraving

To produce engraved or impressed textures, use the point of a sharp knife to sculpt repetitive marks on the surface of heavy-weight cotton paper. Experiment on a piece of scrap paper first, using only the tip of the knife to pick at the paper with just enough pressure to raise a surface texture but not penetrate the paper. Although this is a laborious technique, paper engraving produces wonderfully rich surfaces.

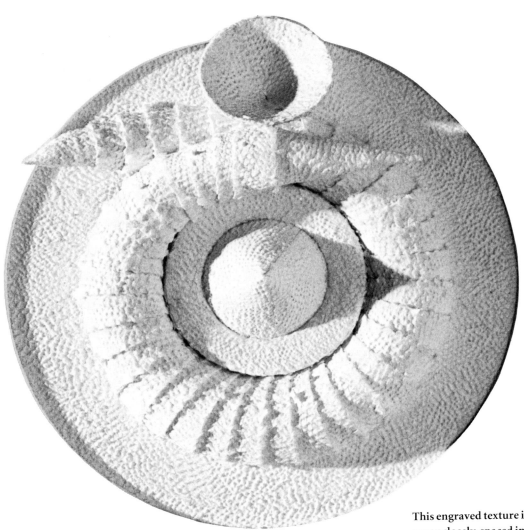

This engraved texture is composed of many closely-spaced incisions that penetrate only the surface of the paper. Angled lighting creates shadow areas that further enhance the surface texture. Vito Capone, *Avvolto*, 1987. Sculpted paper, 19¾ x 23½" (50 x 60 cm). Courtesy the artist.

Joanne Brinkman, *Synapses,* 1991. Paper,
24 x 24" (61 x 61 cm). Courtesy the artist.

Crumpling

Try designing by the crimp, crinkle, crumple, pucker and wrinkle method. Here's a technique in controlled serendipity that produces dramatic visual and tactile surfaces. You'll need various types of papers for this experiment, such as flexible and soft papers, collage tissues, paper towels, napkins and household tissues. Crumpled aluminum foil is easily manipulated with the fingers and may also be used to create dramatic surface textures. Also, search for unusual objects made of paper or cardboard that are already crushed or wrinkled. In addition, you will need some white glue and a panel or piece of cardboard to serve as the background.

The surface of a plane not only defines it but also may be a source of its radiant energy.

JONATHAN BLOCK, JERRY LEISURE, AUTHORS AND EDUCATORS

Experiment 7

Creating a Rhythmic Design

Start by making a preliminary sketch on the background panel. The drawing may simply be a group of lines that divide the overall space into various compartments. Next, crumple the selected papers. Think about design concepts such as repetition, rhythm, focus (center of interest) and a limited color scheme to ensure visual interest. Instead of using a hodge-podge of different textures, select only a few and repeat them. Arrange the majority of the crumpled papers in a particular direction to provide rhythmic alignment. For greater unity, consider using only white papers or papers of a single color along with a paper of contrasting color. Adhere the crumpled papers to the base panel with white glue. Brush glue directly to the undersurface of the crumpled paper. Lightweight crumpled tissues may be dipped into a sticky solution of glue and water (mixed 1:1) and applied to the background.

> *Note:* Color can be used to unify a cluttered composition. You may do this by first brushing the entire composition with black paint. Then dip a brush in a different color of paint, blotting excess on a paper towel. Drag the brush lightly over the textures to produce colorful drybrush effects.

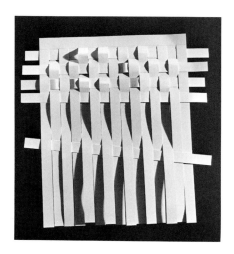

Interesting patterns can be produced by interlacing paper strips. The looms can be made of paper, cardboard or other readily available materials. Papers can also be woven in conventional looms strung with a linen warp.

Weaving

Weaving is the interlacing of warp fibers, or fibers that run length-wise, with the weft fibers, or those that run cross-wise. A loom is a matrix device that anchors and controls the fibers. Paper can be woven in different ways to create unique designs or sculptured forms. These include interlacing paper strips on a paper matrix, interlacing paper strips on a makeshift loom, and weaving paper strips on a standard textile loom.

Experiment 8
A Paper Matrix

By mimicking standard textile loom-weaving techniques, paper strips can be woven in a horizontal/vertical manner on a sheet of perforated paper serving as a matrix. Mark and cut a large sheet of paper to form a matrix for weaving. Begin by marking off spaces one-half to one-inch apart at the top and bottom of the paper. Draw lines to connect the points on opposing sides of the paper, creating a series of parallel lines. Use an X-acto knife and straightedge to cut the lines. Do not cut all the way across the page; rather, leave a one-inch border on one edge to secure the matrix together. You may elect to have a border all around your weaving. To do so, simply fold the sheet of paper in half prior to measuring and cutting. After cutting, open the paper to reveal a matrix that is enclosed by a border.

Cut one-half- to one-inch-wide paper strips and interlace them in an under-over fashion on the matrix to produce an allover pattern. Use strips of alternate colors to provide contrast. Try weaving some strips in a loose or twisted manner, allowing loops to provide a three-dimensional variation to the woven surface pattern.

Experiment 9
Makeshift Looms

Make a cardboard loom with notches on each end (about three notches to the inch) to accommodate a vertical warp of twine. This will provide the matrix for weaving strips of paper. Also experiment with commercially made frame-type looms, which are available from craft supply stores or can be made from old picture frames. A frame loom has finishing nails evenly spaced on two ends that can accommodate a vertical warp of twine.

With a little imagination, practically anything can be pressed into service as a matrix for weaving. A tree branch strung with a spider-web-like warp, for example, would provide a unique matrix. Try using a converted picture frame, a coarse wire mesh screen, window blinds, a gridded plastic lighting panel or other found objects. Interlace and/or stuff the grids with paper strips. Miscellaneous material such as ribbons, laces or rings may be incorporated into the design.

Standard Looms

Use a conventional textile floor loom strung with a linen warp. Produce an unconventional artwork by interlacing a weft of paper strips along with mixed media.

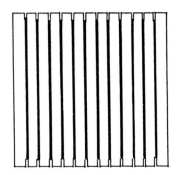
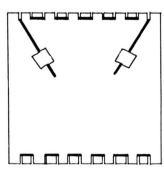

Twine is wound tightly around the notches of a cardboard loom. The beginning and end of the piece of twine are taped to the back of the cardboard loom.

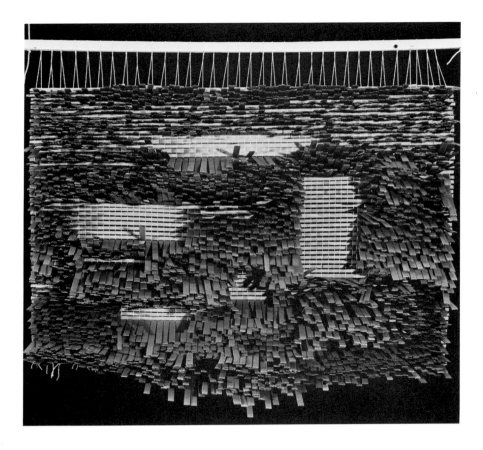

Dieter Kramer, *Interlaced Pattern*, 1990. Paper, cardboard, cord. Courtesy Elisabeth Sinken.

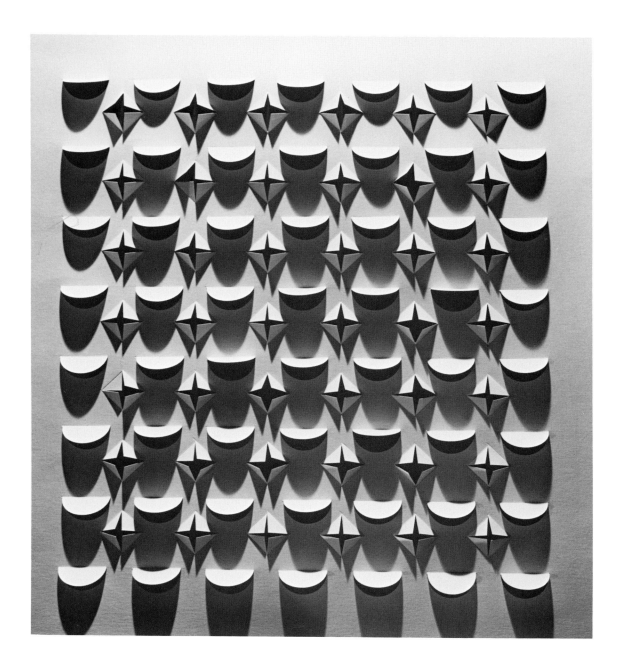

Two modular units alternate to produce a distinctive pattern. Richard Hoesch, *Chiaroscuro*, 1990. Paper, 24 x 24" (61 x 61 cm). Courtesy the artist.

Cut, Crease, Fold and Repeat

Modular tabs—formed by making cuts, creases and folds on flat paper—are light-capturing elements that produce dramatic surface textures when repeated to form allover patterns. Surfaces appear charged with energy, and the resulting low-relief appears as a unified composition of structural and tonal counterchanges.

Light-Capturing Designs

Design your own modular unit to use repeatedly in a unified design. Consider using basic geometric shapes. For more complex designs, repeat basic shapes, one within another, in gradually decreasing size. Rule a sheet of medium-weight paper lightly with pencil to divide the paper into compartments. Next, lightly draw the modular unit inside each compartment. Then, with an X-acto or utility knife, carefully cut designated lines using proper safety precautions. Use a letter opener to rub over fold lines, forming creases as required. Fold each tab to produce a relief effect. Mount the finished work on a sheet of black paper.

Other options: Produce a design that alternates two different modular units or a design in which the tabs have curved planes (roll tabs over a dowel or knitting needle). Also try planning your design within a circular, rather than a rectangular, piece of background paper.

Modular units, each of which could be used for making an allover pattern, were made by cutting, creasing and folding. Dotted lines indicate fold lines.

Patterns for modular units. To follow these patterns, cut on the solid lines, and crease and fold on the dotted lines.

Experiment 12

Make It Stand

In a sense, this experiment is about paper's rite of passage from the flat, two-dimensional realm into three-dimensional space. Here, the basic idea is to transform a sheet of paper—a normally flat, inanimate material—into a three-dimensional stand-up structure that is physically strong and visually dynamic. You can do this by using the basic techniques of creasing, cutting and folding. Once a flat sheet of paper has been dealt with in this manner, it not only stands readily but is capable of supporting a weight surprisingly heavier than itself.

Simple Stand-Up Structures Create a simple stand-up structure made of a folded sheet of paper that has been modulated with cuts, creases and folds. Start by folding a rectangular sheet of medium-weight white paper in half vertically. Place the folded sheet on a pulp-board work surface, and make a series of cuts and creases inward from the spine edge as shown in the illustrations above (dotted lines represent lines to be creased). Next, stand the paper on end and bend the cut-and-creased shapes outward and inward to produce the desired surface modulation.

Pattern for creating a free-standing column. Solid lines indicate cut lines, while dotted lines indicate lines to be creased and folded. Note that a small strip was left along one edge as a tab. Fasten the column together by applying white glue to the end tab.

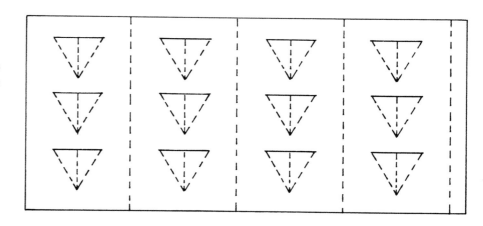

72

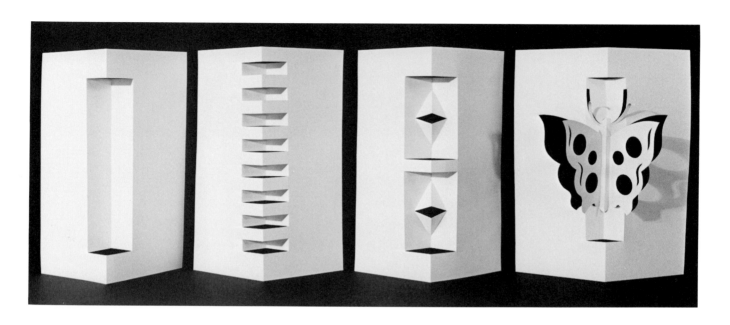

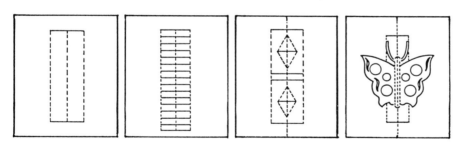

The basic techniques of cutting, creasing and folding are employed to transform paper from a flat material to a spatial structure.

Patterns for creating simple stand-up structures. To follow these patterns, cut on the solid lines, and crease and fold on the dotted lines.

Free-Standing Columns Crease and fold a sheet of paper to produce either a hollow prism, cube or extended cube, but don't yet fasten the seam to hold the shape together. With the form folded, make a series of cuts, creases and folds on the spine edges (the creased sides) of the paper in accordance with your design. Open up the paper flat, stand the paper upright, glue the seam to form a column, then manipulate the cut-and-scored areas to produce spatial counter-changes. To construct a hollow cylinder with a modulated surface pattern, make the cuts and creases on a flat sheet of paper, then curl the paper to form a tube. Staple or tape the seam.

A free-standing column, created by the crease-and-fold method, is crowned with a stellated dodecahedron. Margaret Olsen, *Column*, 1991. Paper, 18 x 4" (46 x 10 cm). Courtesy the artist.

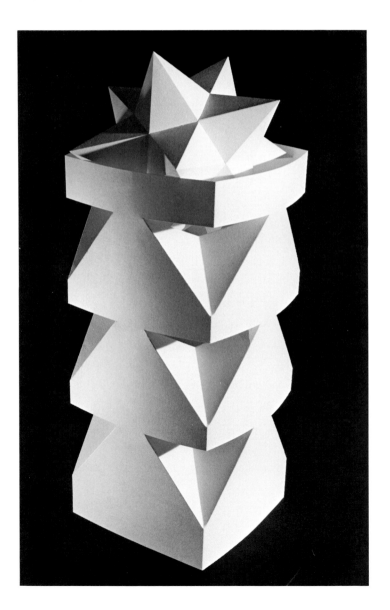

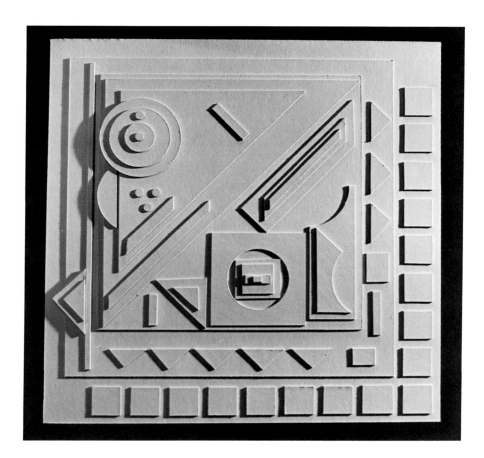

Jason Rogers, *Bas-Relief,* 1990. Cardboard, 18 x 18" (46 x 46 cm). Courtesy the artist.

Relief Sculpture

Experiment 13

Layering Flat Shapes

A low-relief sculpture can be created by gluing flat cardboard shapes onto the surface of a background panel, or the ground plane. When cutout shapes of diminishing size are overlaid, a bas-relief begins to rise from the ground plane, something like the form of a three-dimensional topographical map. The largest shape is glued down first, followed by successively smaller concentric shapes. Best results are obtained with heavy-weight paper such as illustration board or mat board. A handy tool is a circle cutter, available from most art supply stores. Use white glue to attach components.

Low or Bas-Relief With pencil, paper and, if necessary, mechanical drawing instruments, plan a design for a cardboard bas-relief. Draw concentric shapes to indicate the number of elevated "steps." Apply design principles such as contrast (variation of size), repetition and dominance (progression and emphasis).

relief The projection of elements from a ground plane. Relief is of three kinds: high relief (alto-rilievo), low relief (basso-rilievo, or bas-relief) and middle relief (mezzo-rilievo). The distinction lies in the degree of projection.

CENTURY DICTIONARY, NINETEENTH CENTURY ENCYCLOPEDIC LEXICON

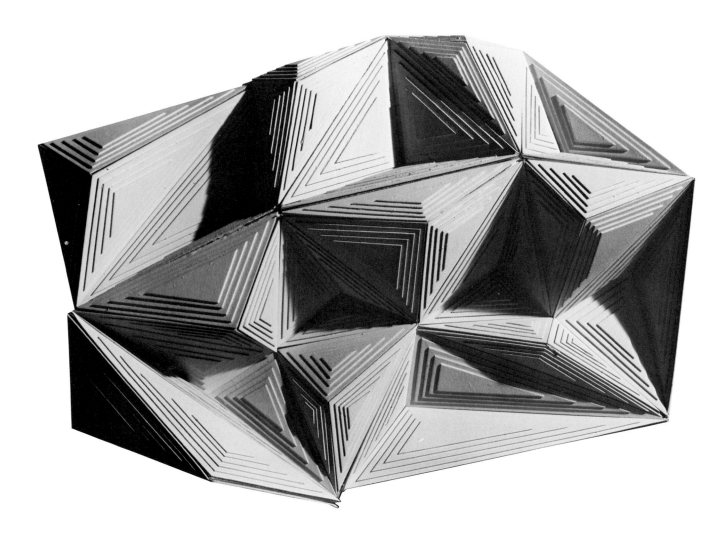

Bas-relief produced by overlayering cardboard on an irregular base. Student work from the Preusser Design course, 1970, Massachusetts Institute of Technology. Courtesy Mr. Preusser. Photo by Nishan Bichajian.

Next, reproduce each shape in your drawing on a piece of white, heavy-weight paper. Cut out each shape with a mat knife, scissors or circle cutter. Then, overlay and glue the shapes in the order specified by your design. Although the bas-relief will be composed only of white-on-white cardboard shapes, the sculptural nature of the work will produce subtle light and shadow effects.

Option: For making figurative or more complex designs, cut the component shapes out of illustration board with a jigsaw, equipped with a fine-tooth blade.

Safety Note: Use care in operating machinery. Follow manufacturer's guidelines at all times, using safety goggles and/or gloves when appropriate.

Experiment 14
Tabs

Cardboard tabs are an effective way of elevating flat, cutout shapes from the ground plane. Make tabs by cutting strips of cardboard. The width of the tabs determines the elevation between cardboard shapes. The length of the tabs should be adjusted according to the size of the shapes being elevated. This is often a trial-and-error process. Score the cardboard in the center lengthwise, and bend to form a V, as shown in the illustration. Position and glue the edges of these tabs to the ground plane with white glue. Create relief by building up layers of shapes, separating them with tabs of varying heights. The tabs will be hidden from frontal view, yet will support and elevate the raised components.

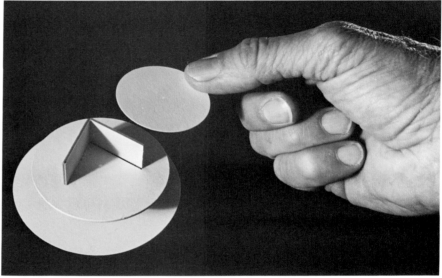

Tabs made of paper or cardboard are glued on their edges and placed between component shapes in high relief.

Ray Fisher, *Victorian House*, 1990. Overlaid cardboard shapes, 32 x 40" (81 x 102 cm). Courtesy the artist.

High Relief Select a medium- or heavy-weight paper or cardboard. Plan an abstract or representational motif to be used as a design for a relief. The high relief should rise a total of one to four inches from the ground plane. With tools such as a mat knife, circle cutter, paper cutter or jig saw, cut out the shapes of the design. Next, make tabs from strips of cardboard that measure one quarter- to one-inch wide, and cut them to a length appropriate for each cardboard shape. Assemble and glue the elements in place beginning with the largest shape first. Place one or more tabs under each shape, attaching it to the preceding shape with white glue. Continue the procedure, attaching progressively smaller shapes, until the high-relief sculpture is complete.

Experiment 15

Strips

Another way of producing low-relief sculpture is with long, narrow, flexible paper strips. The strips are curled and bent, glued on their edges at right angles to a cardboard base, and glued to each other at touch points to form a design. By creating depth and interest with shadows, light, especially oblique light, plays an important role in defining the relief surface. The light and shadow effect is further enhanced if the design is composed of strips of various widths.

Paper strips of various lengths were rolled, bent and folded in accordance with a design. Paper clips hold glued ends together until the adhesive dries.

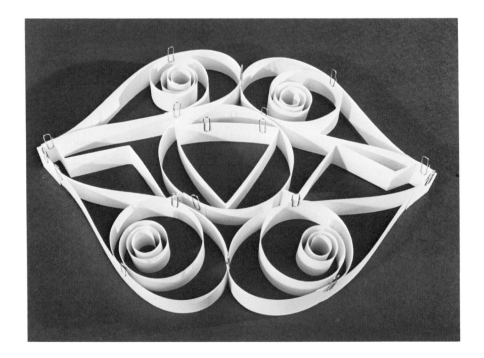

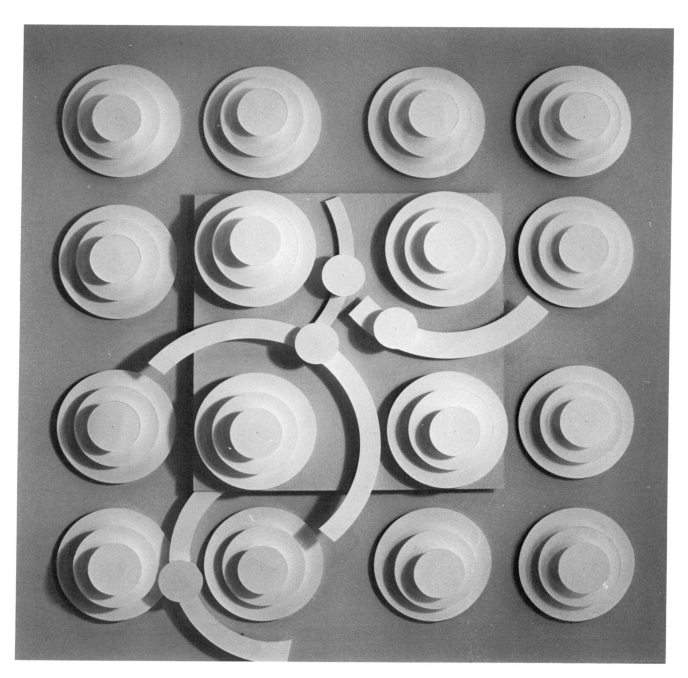

Michael Garcia, *High-Relief Wall Piece*,
1990. Cardboard, 16 x 16" (41 x 41 cm).
Courtesy the artist.

Collage. Margo Lumbry, *Sanibel Sun,*
1991. Paper, 36 x 24" (91 x 61 cm). Courtesy
the artist.

Light-Capturing Relief Plan a simple, stylized design for a low-relief sculpture
featuring a figurative or abstract motif. Start by making a light pencil drawing of
your design on a piece of white cardboard. Next, cut one-half-inch-wide strips
(and other widths as required) from white, medium-weight paper. Use a paper
trimmer or mat knife with a ruler or steel edge to make the strips. Then, cut the
strips to the lengths needed to complete the design. Bend and curl the strips and
glue their edges in place on the ground plane using white glue as an adhesive. If
necessary, use paper clips on the ends of the strips to temporarily hold them
together until the glue sets. The assembly will be easier to work with if you
attach the components in a progressive, concentric order: largest ones first,
mid-size ones next, smallest pieces last.

> *Option*: Choose strips of brightly colored, rather than white, paper to
> glue onto a black or gray background. Try adding collage elements to
> further enhance the design.

Sculpture-in-the-Round

If a picture is worth a thousand words, is a sculpture worth ten thousand pictures? Sculpture-in-the-round is an entity not only in three-dimensional space but in time as well. This means that a three-dimensional construction cannot be totally appreciated from a single viewpoint, but requires the spectator to move around it, gathering other perceptions. Creating sculpture-in-the-round, therefore, is analogous to producing hundreds of drawings in a single artwork; the

Ben Krasner, *Sculpture-in-the-Round,* 1990. Paper, 24 x 12" (61 x 30 cm). Courtesy the artist.

When looking at sculpture we can walk up to it, back away, walk around it, retrace our steps, change our position for a different viewpoint, move in close or to a distance to perceive it as we wish. Not even a three-dimensional film could provide us with this experience.

BERNARD MYERS, CONTEMPORARY WRITER

third dimension means we must consider the sculpture from every direction—from front, back, top and sides—to produce an organized structure.

Experiment 16
Focusing on Composition

Exploit the characteristics of paper as a sculpture medium by cutting and forming a piece of white, medium-weight paper into a variety of shapes and strips. Use techniques such as creasing, folding, rolling and pleating. Arrange the components to provide visual continuity as you view the structure from different angles. Join the components by notching, stapling, taping or gluing. (Use paper clips to hold glued parts together until the adhesive sets.) Because the sculpture will be composed of planar rather than solid shapes, keep in mind the words of Clement Greenberg, a noted author and art critic who, in describing a contemporary direction in sculpture, proclaimed, "Space is there to be shaped, divided and enclosed, but not to be filled." His words underscore the importance of remembering that negative space is equally important as positive form in sculptural composition.

Experiment 17
Adding a New Dimension: Color

Make a sculpture-in-the-round that involves color. Use commercially available colored papers or white paper you have decorated yourself with acrylic paint or other art media and techniques such as painting, dry-brushing, texturing, spraying or stippling. Cut and shape the paper to form a three-dimensional construction.

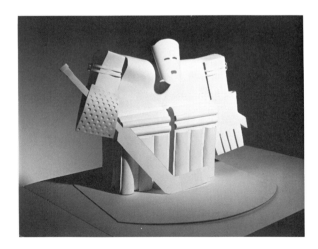

Pleating

Paper is easily pleated by alternately scoring lines on its front and back sides and bending it to form an accordion fold. On patterns developed for pleated forms, solid lines indicate lines that should be creased and folded on the front of the paper; dotted lines indicate lines that should be creased and folded on the back of the paper. If you pay careful attention to accurate measuring and folding, a sheet of paper can be transformed into a distinctive three-dimensional pattern.

Folding a single sheet of paper can give it strength and rhythmical form.

HIROSHI OGAMI, ARTIST AND AUTHOR

Experiment 18
Straight, Parallel Pleats

You will need a medium-weight paper, a ruler, a creasing tool such as a dull knife or letter opener, dividers and a 4H pencil. Determine the grain of the paper and plan the pleats to run parallel to it. Using a ruler and/or dividers, mark off spaces at the top and bottom of the paper, pressing hard enough with the pencil to leave tiny holes on the surface. Draw lines to connect the pinholes on opposing sides of the paper, creating a series of parallel lines. Next, with a straightedge or ruler as a guide, score and crease every other line (shown as continuous lines in the illustrations). Turn the paper over and score and crease the

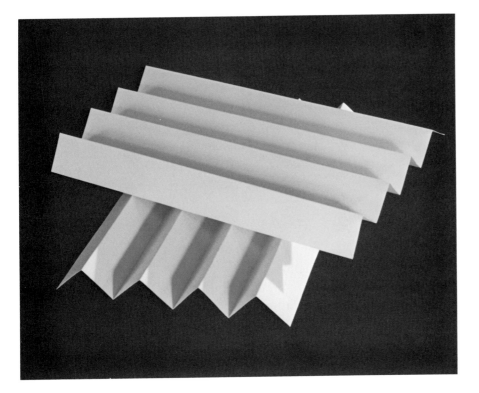

Accordion pleating offers a variety of sculptural effects.

83

remaining lines on the back (the dotted lines in the illustration). Press firmly to make sharp indentations; it will help produce a clean edge. By alternately scoring both sides of the paper, you will be able to fold the paper into clean, accordion-like pleats. Finally, carefully fold the paper on the indentations, one pleat at a time, first the front, then the back until the accordion pattern is produced. Smooth each edge of the pleat with the creaser as you proceed.

Curved and Zig-Zag Pleats

Try making pleats with curved and zig-zag patterns. Use a compass to draw even curves, or create a curved cardboard template from which parallel curved lines can be traced. Score as with straight, parallel pleats. Creasing and folding must be done carefully to retain the curved shapes. For zig-zag patterns, follow the above procedure using angled, zig-zag lines instead of curves. In both cases, the diagrams provided will help plan your design.

Patterns for creating straight, curved and zig-zag pleats. Solid lines should be creased and folded on the front of the paper, while dotted lines should be creased and folded on the back.

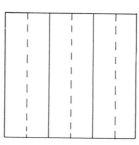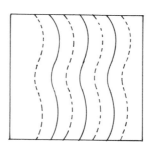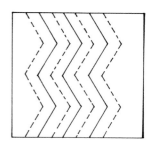

Pattern for constructing *Zig-Zag Bas-Relief*. Solid lines indicate lines that should be creased and folded on the front of the paper; dotted lines should be creased and folded on the back of the paper.

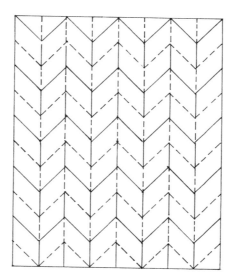

Opposite:
Try making a relief or three-dimensional structure that incorporates a zig-zag pleated pattern. Florence Temko, *Zig-Zag Bas-Relief*, 1989. Paper. Courtesy the artist.

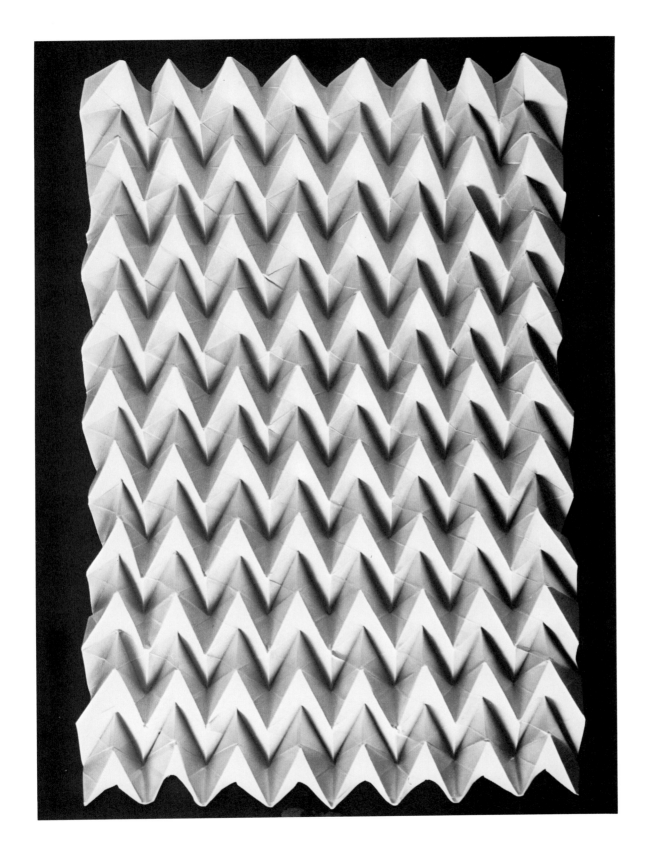

Bow-shaped pleated designs were
produced by constricting the pleated
forms at their midpoints. Carolyn A. Dahl,
Pleated Rhythms, 1989. Dyed paper, 11 x 17"
(28 x 43 cm). Courtesy the artist.

A variety of bas-relief designs can be constructed from creased and folded sculptural forms.

87

Low-Relief Pleated Design

Pleated paper can be cut to create shapes other than that of the original, usually rectangular, paper. These shapes can then be arranged on a background for further design possibilities. Plan a low-relief design that features, or is totally composed of, an accordion-pleat pattern. Draw the guidelines on medium-weight paper with a hard-lead pencil. Crease the lines with sufficient pressure to make a deep indentation in the paper. Erase the pencil lines prior to folding.

Lamp design. Heavy-weight flexible paper, treated with fire retardant and pleated to form faceted spheres, can be used to fashion lamp shades and other objects for applied design.

Pleated forms are dominant elements in this complex paper sculpture. Leo Monahan, *Symbiosis.* Paper, air-brushed color. Courtesy the artist.

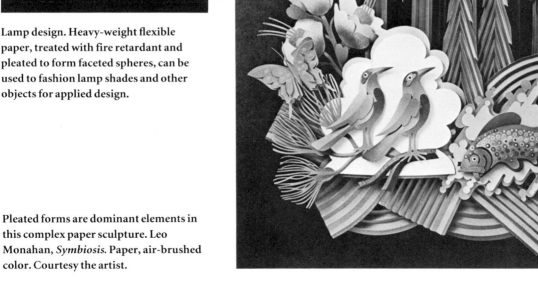

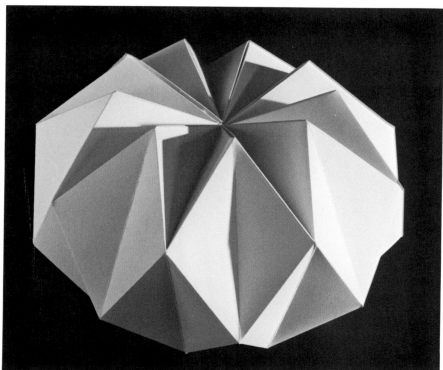

This faceted sphere is made up of vertical and diagonal pleating.

Diagram for constructing the faceted sphere. The vertical lines are alternately creased on the front and back sides of the paper; solid lines indicate lines that should be creased on the front, while dotted lines should be creased on the back. Both sets of diagonal lines are creased on the back side, as shown by the dotted lines. The pleated paper is folded and compressed and the two ends taped together. The compressed form becomes spherical and holds its shape with the aid of heavy string threaded through the punched holes and tied at both the top and bottom.

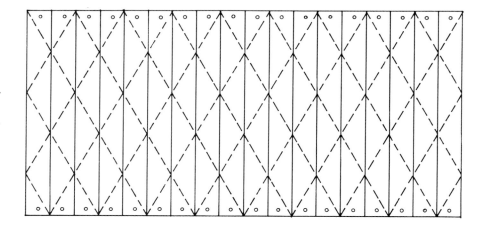

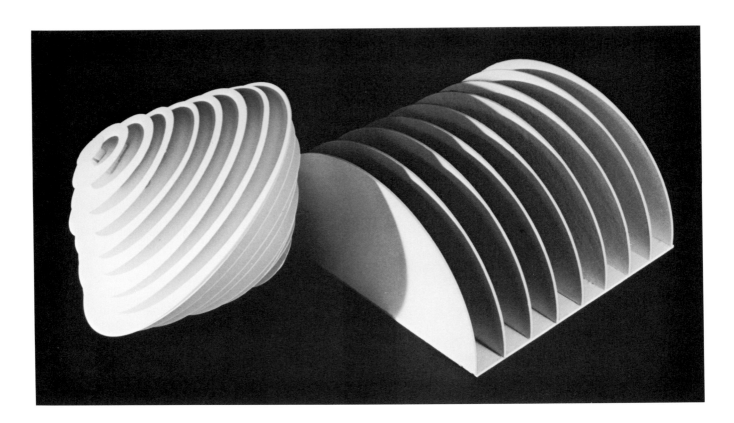

Sculptural volume is expressed by closely
spaced cardboard planes. They can be
used to imply a variety of forms,
depending on whether the planes are of
equal or graduated size.

Implied Volume

The traditionalist's notion of sculpture centers on the idea of space being dis-
placed by solid form. Michelangelo, for example, produced his works by carving
massive chunks of marble to "liberate" images that he mentally projected into
the stone. In his work, sculptural volume is real, the stone is solid to the core.
On the other hand, sculpture also deals with implied volume, wherein negative
space becomes an important factor. To clarify the concept of implied volume,
picture a solid block of clay that is cut into slabs, like slices of cheese. Now imagine the slabs separated and standing a few inches apart from each other. Volume
is no longer composed of a single, solid form, but rather of separate elements
that are optically linked to present the illusion of a volumetric form.

Repeated Planes

Using heavy-weight paper or cardboard, assemble planar shapes to produce the effect of implied volume. First, imagine cross sections of a particular volumetric form, as if it were sliced like a loaf of bread. Determine the repetitive planes you will need to produce an equivalent form based on implied volume. To make an implied cube, for example, you would only need to space apart identical square shapes, while to create an implied sphere or pyramid you would need to repeat and space apart shapes that are similar, yet graduated in size. Draw the necessary shapes on the paper or cardboard and cut them out. To assemble the sculpture, separate and glue together the planar shapes with cardboard tabs. Note that closely spaced planes emphasize the volumetric effect while planes placed further apart will diminish it.

> *Option:* Try making interpenetrating forms out of two or more implied-volume sculptures. An implied cube, for example, could be combined with an implied sphere, etc.

The peculiarity of sculpture as an art is that it creates a three-dimensional object in space. We may say that for the painter space is a luxury; for the sculptor it is a necessity.

SIR HERBERT READ, TWENTIETH CENTURY ENGLISH WRITER

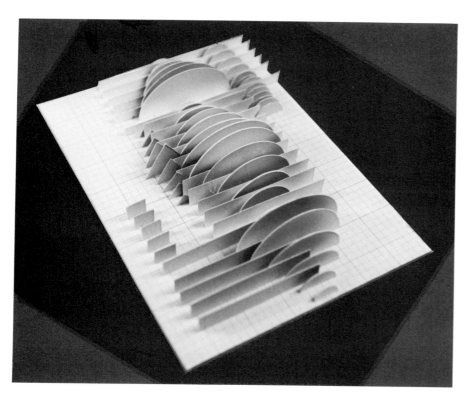

Pavlos, *Nature Morte*, 1981. Paper, 16 x 13¾ x 13¾" (41 x 35 x 35 cm). Courtesy Redmann Gallery, Berlin.

Barbara Brown, *Interpenetrating Forms*. Cardboard. Courtesy the artist.

Open Forms

The Constructivist movement of the 1920s triggered a radical change in sculpture. The use of monolithic, representational form, such as in the work by Michelangelo, gave way to open, geometric structures without figurative representation.

In essence, sculpture is interaction between form and space. In open-form structures, space predominates; it has claimed a major victory in its interplay with form. The structures tend to be skeletal, light and airy. Open form could be called introverted, since sculptural variations lie principally within the work. Conversely, closed-form structures tend to be solid and weighty in appearance; interior space is shut off and variations lie only on the surface of the sculpture.

Experiment 22

Flat Shapes

Select a geometric shape such as a triangle, circle or square, and cut out five to ten repetitive units, each one progressively smaller in size. Use medium- or heavy-weight paper (or cardboard) and a mat knife or circle cutter to make the

Elisabeth Sinken, *Flat Planes Become Spatial,* **1990. Cardboard. Courtesy the artist.**

This open-form, skeletal icosahedron was produced by removing the interior spaces of the pattern prior to folding.

shapes. Cut and remove the interior portion of each flat shape to create a more open, skeletal structure as shown at right. Fit the units inside each other at alternating angles to produce a three-dimensional structure. Apply glue at touch points to adhere the shapes to one another. Notch some of the edges to join the shapes if desired. (See Joining by Notching, page 33.)

Experiment 23
Polyhedra

Refer to the patterns for making basic polyhedral forms, or forms composed of plane faces, that appear on pages 44 to 53. Before folding a pattern, use a mat knife to remove a large portion of the interior space, as in the illustration at right, so that the resulting shapes will be skeletal rather than solid when folded and assembled.

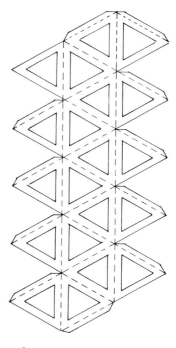

Pattern for constructing the skeletal icosahedron. Solid lines indicate cut lines. (Note that interior cut lines should be made with an X-acto knife and straight edge, while exterior lines may be cut with a scissors, if desired.) Crease and fold on the dotted lines, and apply glue to the tabs for fastening.

Square shapes cut from cardboard were notched and interlocked to produce this modular construction.

modular adj*mäj-ə-lər*\ *2: constructed with standardized units or dimensions for flexibility and variety in use.*

WEBSTER'S NINTH NEW COLLEGIATE DICTIONARY

Modules

A module is an individual unit of construction. Everything in our world is made up of modular units. Nature has ninety-two different elements, each with its own atomic structure, which are the building blocks—or modules—for all that nature produces. In the world of art, a module that repeats becomes a creative system for determining the shape and substance of a work, whether in sculpture, architecture, painting or furniture design. The artist invents with modules through the processes of grouping and serializing.

Experiment 24
Flat Shapes

Select a basic geometric shape such as a triangle, square, circle, pentagon or hexagon to serve as a modular unit. Cut twenty or more identical shapes from heavy-weight paper and notch each shape as shown at right. (Refer to directions for notching, page 33.) Join the units to produce a unified three-dimensional structure.

> *Option:* Select two different geometric shapes and combine them to produce a three-dimensional construction.

Patterns for constructing notched modular units.

Experiment 25
Solid Units

Refer to pages 44 to 53, which describe polyhedral forms. Select one of the volumetric forms to serve as a modular unit. With the aid of the pattern, construct five to ten forms and glue them together to produce an architectural structure. Try various arrangements of the modular units before gluing them.

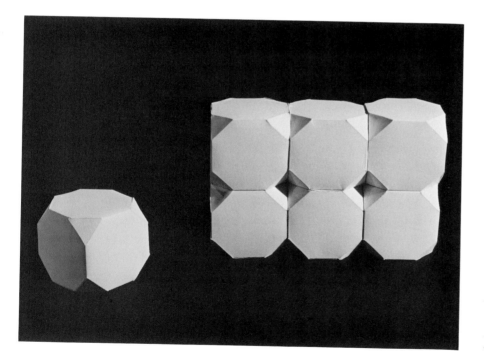

Solid modular units can be joined to produce architectural structures. The truncated hexahedron is among the polyhedral forms that can be used for this purpose.

Imagination, as it is too often misunderstood, is mere fantasy, the image-making power, common to all who have the gift of dreams.

JOHN MILTON, SEVENTEENTH CENTURY ENGLISH POET

Merging Form with Fantasy

"Besides the actual universe," wrote J.M. Synge, a poet and leading figure in the nineteenth century Irish literary renaissance, "I can see in my imagination other universes in which the laws are different." Guided by such daring, the Dutch-born artist M.C. Escher created puzzling and often bizarre optical illusions that contravene the laws of nature and normal perception, yet delight the senses. His work evokes a surrealistic flavor of unreality because geometric structures—which have the air of rationality—are interplayed with absurd, dream-like imagery. Potent imagery is always generated when contrasts between order and chaos, the normal and abnormal, and the real and surreal are interlocked.

"Two chameleons . . . cling by their legs and tails to the beams of their cage as it swirls through space." M.C. Escher, from *M.C. Escher, The Graphic Work,* published by Benedikt Taschen, 1990. *Stars,* 1948. Wood engraving, 12½ x 10" (32 x 26 cm). © 1948 M.C. Escher/Cordon Art-Baarn-Holland.

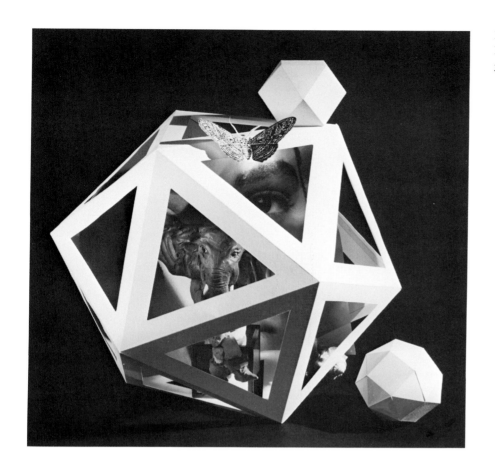

Experiment 26

Surreal Constructions

Refer to the geometric shapes and patterns that appear on pages 49 to 53. Construct one of the shapes in medium-weight paper to serve as the "rational" element in a surreal, three-dimensional construction. Before assembling the pattern, you may wish to cut out the inside area of each plane so the interior space of the assembled shape will be visible. Create a surreal image by assembling disparate collage and found objects inside and around the geometric shape. Make the sculpture humorous or bizarre. Topple mental and sensory expectations by forcing opposite and seemingly contrary ideas and objects to fit together. Keep in mind the words of Jean-Jacques Rousseau, the noted eighteenth century French philosopher: "The world of reality has its limits but the world of imagination is boundless. Not being able to enlarge the one, let's contract the other!"

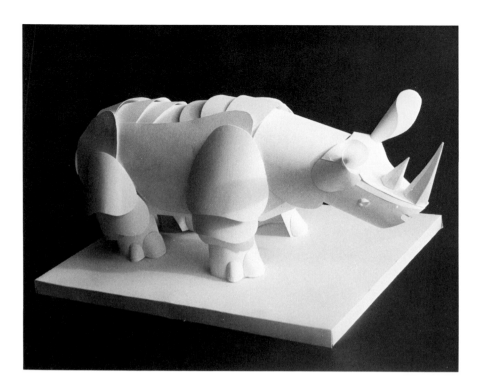

Student work from the Alberta College of Art, *Rhino,* 1980. Paper, 10 x 3" (25 x 8 cm). Courtesy Ken Samuelson.

Stylizing the Subject

To *stylize* is to design according to a personal manner of working rather than according to nature. This notion is reflected in the work of Paul Klee, the acclaimed artist and teacher of Germany's Bauhaus school of design, who acknowledged nature as the greatest source of artistic inspiration but admonished his students against slavish imitation. "One should not imitate nature, but rather look through nature to seek the essence rather than the appearance of things," said Klee.

Unlike the camera, which records every detail, artists select only details pertinent to their artistic vision. They simplify, substitute, omit, compress and recombine visual information to make perceptions of nature less complicated. In short, artists edit what they see. The art medium itself—in this instance, paper—becomes a cooperative factor as artists translate the reality of nature into an "aesthetic reality."

Simplifying Nature

Select a subject from nature—the image of a human face or figure, a bird, fish, horse, butterfly, flower, tree, etc.—to serve as a motif for a paper sculpture. Make preliminary sketches from life or detailed photographs. Simplify the shapes and forms of your subject; reduce the image toward geometric stylization and basic geometric shapes such as circles, squares, triangles, cubes, cylinders and cones. Use medium-weight paper and tools such as an X-acto or utility knife and scissors, along with techniques such as creasing, folding, rolling, curling, pleating and joining to produce a bas-relief or free-standing sculpture.

Safety Note: Use proper safety precautions when working with knives and other sharp tools.

Leo Monahan, *Birds of a Feather.* **Paper, air-brushed color. Courtesy the artist.**

Basket format. Carolyn A. Dahl, *Confetti Cloud Sticks.* Dyed paper with painted sticks, 8 x 15" (20 x 38 cm). Courtesy the artist.

Exploring Format

Experiment 28

Baskets

Although baskets are generally considered utilitarian objects, with poetic license, they can be perceived as potent vehicles for symbolic expression. Metaphorically, the mind is a basket, a receptacle of knowledge and experience, a receiving vessel of stimuli and emotions, and the container of hopes, fears and fantasies. In the art-making context, artists can use the basket format to express this powerful symbolism with biographical imagery imparted on dynamic three-dimensional designs.

Basket Designs Design a paper sculpture that explores the possibilities of the basket format. Work with papier-mâché pulp or strips. (See Papier-Mâché, pages 112–113.) Papier-mâché can be layered over or inside a bowl, plaster form or other shape acting as a mold. Incorporate designs and other elements (such as color and other surface embellishments) inside and outside the form in accordance with an idea or inspiration. Combine materials to realize an idea or emotion, or to make a narrative statement.

Various commercial papers, woven on a floor loom strung with linen warp, have been formed into a basket. Mizuhiki is a paper cord from Japan that is also used as weft. Diane Sheehan, *Black Light*, 1989. Paper, linen, mizuhiki, 19 x 19 x 9" (48 x 48 x 23 cm). Courtesy the artist.

Although baskets appear to reveal all their functions and meanings, they can also be secretive, enclosing and hiding information. Some of my works are like lidless treasure boxes. I collect in them very personal responses to my environment.

CAROLYN DAHL, ARTIST

My books are diaries, a metaphor for my life. They are containers for fragments of ideas and images, notes and anecdotes, wishes and secrets; they suggest time compressed, the marriage of art and craft, ritual and a sense of energy, motion and process.

LOIS POLANSKY, ARTIST

Book format (pages turn). Sandra Jackman, *Send in the Clowns.* **Paper, paint, collage, found objects, 4 x 4 x 2" (10 x 10 x 5 cm). Courtesy the artist.**

Experiment 29

Books

Artists' books are generally mixed-media artworks that allow their creators to freely combine design, drawing, graphics, painting, collage and found materials—as well as words or letters. Like literary works, artists' books are created for purposes of documenting, enlightening, mystifying and/or entertaining. They can comprise abstract designs and visual elements calculated to delight the eye or present metaphoric images intended to stimulate the mind through symbolic inference. In the hands of the artist-punster, the book genre can be used to present a preposterous idea or visual joke. Contemporary artists favor books as a means for expressing biographical information. Franz Kafka, the early twentieth century Austrian writer known for his darkly surrealistic works, once noted: "Many a book is like a key to unknown chambers within the castle of one's own self."

102

Designing a Book Book formats include pages in loose-leaf binders, accordion-folded pages (foldouts), pages in slip cases or boxes, scrolls and pages with pop-ups or flaps. For loose-leaf books, artwork is hole-punched and bound in a ring binder or with O-rings. Accordion-folded pages are either creased and folded or taped end to end to fold out in a zig-zag manner. Artwork on loose pages can be encased in a cardboard or wooden box to form a slip case format. Scrolls are single-page books that are rolled into a tube shape. For pop-up books, artwork is designed to pop out of the book as it is opened.

Select one of the formats listed above. Use commercially available and/or hand-made papers, along with mixed media and selected paper sculpture techniques to produce a book. Use the format to explore design, voice an opinion, create a biography, or delve into fantasy or comedy.

Book formats include (clockwise from left) accordion-folded, loose-leaf, slip case and pop-ups.

Sculptural books (clockwise from upper left): 1) foldout format, 2) tunnel or peep-show format (a variation of the accordion book), 3, 4) flap format. Work by students of Clem Pennington, Florida International University.

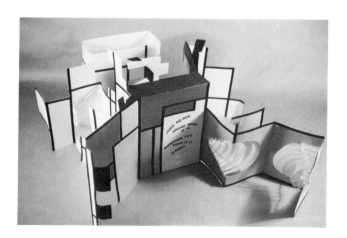

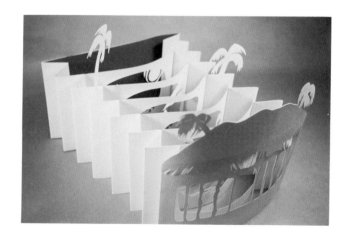

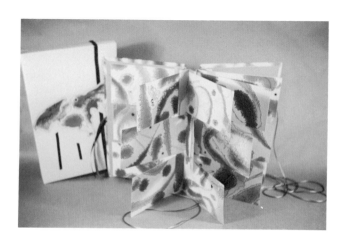

Experiment 30

Tableaux

The term *tableau* denotes a way of organizing sculptural components on a "table," platform or base. The format establishes a spatial boundary on the ground plane, much as the picture frame establishes boundaries in two-dimensional art. The base is an arena for spatial interaction, excluding space and objects around the sculpture.

The word *tableau* is derived from the French phrase *tableau vivant* ("the living picture"), which describes a three-dimensional presentation popular in the early nineteenth century. Costumed performers froze in motionless poses to depict scenes of actual events, usually paraphrasing classic pictorial works such as Leonardo da Vinci's *Last Supper*. In contemporary usage, the word *tableau* is not normally given to mean "theater." The tableau format in visual art employs surrogate "actors" in the form of objects and images arranged on the base plane. Perhaps the best known tableau of the twentieth century is Swiss artist Alberto Giacometti's *The Palace at 4 AM* (1932–33), which is an assemblage of wood, glass and wire shapes arranged on a base. Historian H.W. Janson poignantly describes Giacometti's work: "The airy cage is a three-dimensional equivalent of a Surrealist picture; it creates its own spatial environment that clings to it as though this eerie miniature world were protected from everyday reality by an invisible glass bell."

Tableau Designs   Use the tableau format in one of two ways: 1) Create an abstract high-relief composition, or 2) Create a representational, symbolic or surrealistic motif. If you use the first, non-objective approach, think of the tableau as a device for exploring space and form. Use cut-paper, free-form shapes made from heavy-weight and miscellaneous papers, along with geometric shapes such as circles, squares or triangles. Arrange and glue the components horizontally, vertically or diagonally on a base to form a three-dimensional composition. Avoid unsightly glue lines by applying white glue sparingly to the edges of the shapes that are positioned perpendicularly to the base. Shapes that are horizontally aligned to the base may be raised with cardboard tabs. (See Tabs, page 77.) In using approach number two, glue paper cutouts on a base, combining abstract and figurative elements in accordance with an idea, story or surrealistic fantasy.

Jason Wheeler, *Abstract Tableau,* 1988. Cardboard, 24 x 15 x 8" (61 x 38 x 20 cm). Courtesy the artist.

Alberto Giacometti, *The Palace at 4 AM,* 1932–33. Construction in wood, glass, wire and string, 25 x 28 ¼ x 15 ¾" (63.5 x 72 x 40 cm). Collection The Museum of Modern Art, New York. Purchase.

All the world's a stage.

WILLIAM SHAKESPEARE (1564–1616),
FROM HIS PLAY *AS YOU LIKE IT*

Paul Kwan, *Stage Set Design.* **Paper,
cardboard. Courtesy the artist.**

Experiment 31

Stage Sets

In the performing arts, the word *stage* means a floor or platform for performances. In modern theater, the stage is an architectural structure that includes the proscenium, the proscenium arch, wings, borders, curtains and border lights, all of which are essential to its overall structure. Aside from this physical structure, you need only three things in theater: the play, the actors and the audience.

The visual artist's version of the theatrical stage set is paraphrased, miniaturized and stylized: the "play" is the idea or concept to be communicated and the "actors" are the design elements that compose the work. In a way, the stage-set format is an extension of the tableau model, except that an effort is often made to incorporate features such as borders, wings, curtains and the proscenium arch. This format can also include the peep-box, an artwork enclosed within a box that provides a small opening on one end for viewing. On a much larger scale, the stage-set format can be used for producing site-specific installation art in gallery settings.

Designing a Set Use the stage-set format to make a three-dimensional sculpture. Choose a portion of a play, book or song to portray, or think up a concept that can be successfully portrayed in a stage setting. Then use paper, cardboard, mixed media and paper sculpture techniques to create geometric or figurative elements that reflect the concept you would like to convey. Arrange and attach the elements to a base. Add some of the theater's architectural features such as the proscenium arch, wings and curtains. Use color and selected media as desired.

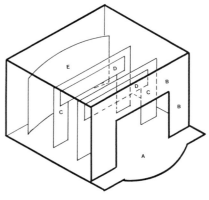

Theater design can serve as an inspiration for the stage-set format. Consider including some of the elements of a formal theater in your design: A. proscenium; B. proscenium arch; C. legs; D. borders; E. cyclorama (painted background).

Stage-set format. Margeret Prentice, *Passing Messages to the Birds,* 1983. Handmade paper, acrylic color, 22 x 25 x 6" (56 x 64 x 15 cm). Courtesy the artist.

Henri Matisse, *Nuit de Noel,* Paris, summer–autumn 1952. Stained-glass window commissioned by *Life,* 1952. Metal framework, 11' ¾" x 4' 6 ¾" x ⅝" (337 x 139 x 2 cm). Executed in the workshop of Paul and Adeline Bony, under the artist's supervision. Collection The Museum of Modern Art, New York. Gift of Time Inc.

The contemporary artist boldly uses the most recognizable quotations. He deliberately encourages the viewer to participate in discovering the genesis of the work.

JEAN LIPMAN, RICHARD MARSHALL, IN THE BOOK *ART ABOUT ART*

Paraphrase a Painting

The word *paraphrase* means to restate or translate. It is a useful technique in art, literature or science as a way of reinventing an old idea. Artists throughout history have borrowed from their predecessors. An example is Paul Cezanne's *Modern Olympia*, which is actually a reinvented version of Edouard Manet's *Olympia*. Since Cezanne's interpretation of Manet's work, there have been countless other "Olympias" by contemporary artists. Other masterworks that have been paraphrased include *The Birth Of Venus* (Sandro Botticelli), *American Gothic* (Grant Wood), *The Last Supper* (Leonardo da Vinci), *The Shriek* (Edvard Munch) and *Nude Descending a Staircase* (Marcel Duchamp). Images from advertising art and comics have also been sources of inspiration for contemporary artists such as Roy Lichtenstein, Tom Wesselmann, Joe Tilson and Eduardo Paolozzi.

In paraphrasing works of art, the artist may take poetic license to change certain design qualities of the source image or to interpret it in a completely different medium. The artist may also choose to place the subject matter in a new context or time frame or to use it for satire or comedy.

Bernice Hansen, *Homage to Matisse*, 1985. Paper, 16 x 12" (41 x 30 cm). Courtesy the artist.

Experiment 32
Transforming the Image

Transform the image from a well-known painting or graphic representation into a bas-relief sculpture. Remember that in paraphrasing a work of art, the idea is not to copy the work directly, but to interpret it. Use poetic license to simplify, or otherwise change the work you choose in order to add a new twist or make an artistic or political statement. Consider whether you want your work to look much like the original or significantly different. Use medium-weight white paper, a piece of cardboard for the base, and scissors, mat knife and other necessary tools. Simplify the shapes of the source image as you translate each component. Use paper sculpture techniques such as creasing, scoring, bending and rolling. Arrange and glue the components onto a cardboard base starting with the largest forms first, followed by those of smaller dimension. Use cardboard tabs to separate the elements. (See Tabs, page 77.)

Using Armatures

Sculptures produced by the armature method are in essence composed of "skin-and-bones." An armature is a substructure that can be made of wire, metal rods, wood, bamboo, reed or any strong skeletal material. The various elements of the substructure are joined according to the type of material used; they may be glued, tied, soldered, welded or wound together to produce a strong armature for the application of paper. Like the design of Japanese lanterns and parasols, thin tissue paper is applied over the armature. The thickness and strength of the skin is determined by the number of layers, or laminae, applied. The resultant sculptural forms are lightweight, vulnerable and translucent.

Charles Escott, *Birdman*. Handcast paper, wood, thread on aluminum panel, 22 x 44" (56 x 12 cm). Courtesy the artist.

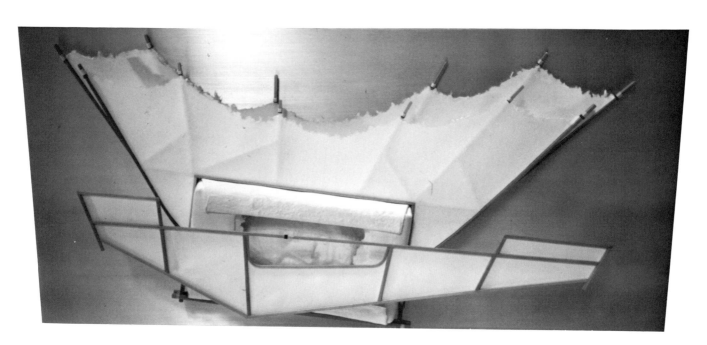

Experiment 33
Laminating Paper

Create a substructure from wire, wood, split bamboo or other pertinent material. Galvanized wires such as 17-gauge electric fence wire and 20-gauge utility wire are flexible and excellent for delineating three-dimensional forms. Use a smaller gauge wire for details, and make sure the wires or other armature components are securely fastened to withstand the light tension that will be exerted by the applied paper shrinking as it dries. Use thin Japanese paper or strong tissue, such as wrapping paper available from department stores, to cover the armature. Cut or tear paper into manageable pieces, about four inches square. Dilute white glue with water (about 1:1) and brush the surface of each paper with the mixture before transferring it to the armature. Stretch the glue-soaked pieces over and around the skeleton. Apply three to five layers of tissue to build up a strong skin. If color is desired, brush the paper with thinned acrylic paint before attaching it to the frame.

Handmade paper may also be applied to the armature. In this instance, sheets of paper are made with the mold and deckle (see Casting, page 117). Apply half-wet sheets of handmade paper over the armature. Overlap them to cover the surface. As the paper dries it will shrink slightly to produce a drum-tight surface.

Frances Semple, *Horse*, 1991. Paper over wire structure, 14 x 20" (36 x 51 cm). Courtesy the artist, Provenance Gallery, Calgary.

Papier-Mâché

You need only a few basic tools and materials to enjoy making papier-mâché sculpture. Using the layer method, required materials include light-weight paper torn into small pieces, an adhesive solution for dipping the torn paper and a mold, armature or previously modeled sculpture upon which to build a shell. Using the pulp method, paper pulp is used instead of paper strips as the laminae.

Depending on the mold or armature used, either the indirect or direct technique may be employed. In the indirect process, a sculpture is first modeled in clay, followed by the application of pulp or five to ten paper layers to produce the shell. When the shell is completely dry, it is cut in half and removed from the clay, then reassembled to form a hollow papier-mâché replica of the original clay sculpture. In the direct method, pulp or paper laminae are applied over a form made of chicken wire or other materials such as wood, expanded metal, Styrofoam, assembled boxes, wadded-up and tied paper or found objects. The armature remains inside the completed sculpture after the laminae are applied to the surface.

Pat Strakowski, *The Flying Lesson.* **Papier-mâché. Courtesy the artist.**

Experiment 34
Layer Method

The most common materials for making papier-mâché sculpture are newsprint, paper towels and grocery bags. Depending on the intended size and configuration of your sculpture, tear the paper into manageable pieces, about one-inch square for smaller forms. Dip the pieces into an adhesive solution such as acrylic polymer medium, mixed one part water with two parts polymer, or white glue, thinned one-to-one with water. Apply the sticky paper to the surface of the clay form or armature. To make a papier-mâché shell that is about ⅛" thick, overlay eight to ten layers of paper. By tearing the paper rather than cutting it, you'll get a feathered edge, which in turn will produce a smoother surface. Also, by alternating the color or type of paper used for each successive lamina, you'll be able to keep track of each layer as it is completed, ensuring an overall even thickness. To make the laminae, dip each torn piece of paper into the glue mixture, then drag them lightly over the edge of the container to remove surplus adhesive before transferring to the mold or clay. It is not necessary to wait for each laminae to dry before applying the next; if time permits, you may apply all the layers in a single session.

For modeling complicated shapes, try soaking facial tissues in the adhesive solution then compressing them to form a clay-like material that can be modeled directly on the papier-mâché surface. Allow the finished sculpture to dry for about a week before painting or decorating it.

> *Note:* For an extra-smooth surface, apply several coats of acrylic gesso to the finished papier-mâché form, sanding lightly between coats. Acrylic paints are ideal for painting and decorating finished objects. As a protective surface, apply a coat of clear varnish.

Experiment 35
Pulp Method

In this method, paper is broken down to a cottage cheese-like consistency and used as a modeling material. Pulp can be made from recycled papers or obtained commercially in premixed form. Apply pulp directly over an armature or into a prepared mold, or model it over a flat, wood panel.

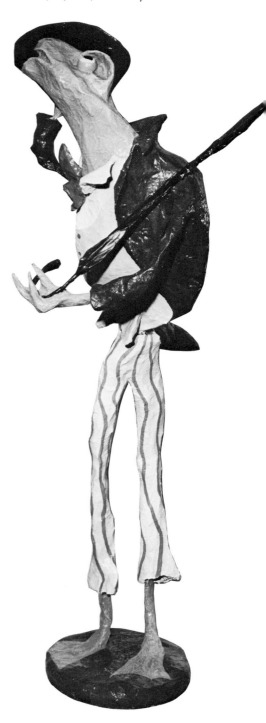

Peter Smith, *Singing Frog,* 1984. Papier-mâché, 6' (1.8 m). Courtesy the artist.

Wearable Masks

The wearable mask conceals identity, yet at the same time "unmasks" the wearer's alter ego for playacting. It is, therefore, popular for drama events and it inspires imagination in myth-making, fantasy, satire, magic and comedy. Generally, papier-mâché masks are made by the indirect process, i.e., a sculpture is first modeled in clay, then layers of paper built over it to form a shell that is removed and decorated. (See page 113.) The half-mask covers only the upper portion of the face, not the mouth, allowing greater flexibility for movement and speech.

Wearable half-mask. Geoff Gerwing, *Creature with Ears,* 1990. Papier-mâché. Courtesy the artist.

Experiment 36
Full-Face Masks

Start by cutting out the basic silhouette shape of a mask from corrugated cardboard or railroad board. Measure and cut eye holes, then glue additional cardboard shapes to the mask surface to define the facial features. For high relief, glue cardboard shapes on end. String or rope may also be adhered to the surface to define facial or design features. Next, apply papier-mâché laminae over the entire surface to integrate the various elements and to develop sculptural form. For details, use facial tissues dipped in a solution of white glue and water and compressed into a clay-like mixture. Allow the mask to dry, then paint and decorate it with acrylic colors. Finally, add other materials or objects for further embellishment. An elastic cord attached to the mask will keep it in place on the wearer's head.

Experiment 37
Casting from Life

Explore this technique by making a half-mask. First, make a plaster mold of the upper portion of a person's face. Consult the bibliography for book references regarding procedures for life casting. Next, paint a release agent such as liquid soap over the wet plaster mold to ensure easy release of the mask, and layer papier-mâché into the mold. Allow the mask to dry, release it from the mold, then paint and decorate it as desired.

Experiment 38
Using Clay Forms

On a plywood work surface, fashion a bas-relief sculpture of your face with water- or oil-base clay. Press lightweight aluminum foil over the modeled clay relief, then apply five to eight papier-mâché laminae over it. (The foil will

Arnold Iger and Paul Kwan, *Mask*, 1990.
Papier-mâché. Courtesy the artists.

1   2   3   4

Full-face mask: 1) Cut out the basic shape from corrugated cardboard. 2) Determine the location of eye holes. 3) Glue three-dimensional shapes to the mask surface to define the nose, mouth and other facial features. 4) Apply papier-mâché laminae over the entire surface to integrate surface elements. When dry, the mask can be decorated with acrylic paint, curled paper and other miscellaneous materials.

1   2   3   4

Half-mask: 1) Develop a likeness of a person's face by either casting from life or modeling in clay. 2) Additional decorative elements may be added with clay. Cover the entire surface with aluminum foil. 3) Small (2 x 2") papier-mâché strips made of kraft paper, old cotton sheets and paper towelling are alternately laminated over the foil. For the smoothest finish, the final layer should be paper towelling. 4) Allow the mask to dry for twenty-four hours. Decorate with acrylic paint, and punch holes in the sides of the mask to attach an elastic head support. Felt or foam padding may be added to the interior of the mask for comfort.

  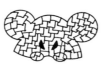 

1   2   3   4

Wire-formed mask: 1) Fashion the outline of a mask using heavy, flexible wire. Add eye holes and additional features with wire, and attach to the basic shape with finer wire and masking tape. 2) Wind masking tape around the wire to hold it together and to cover sharp edges. 3) Apply papier-mâché laminae of opaque paper or colored tissues. 4) When dry, the surface may be decorated.

ensure easy release of the mask from the clay.) Allow the mask to dry, then remove it from the form. Decorate with acrylic colors and materials such as sequins, beads, feathers, glitter and junk jewelry. The mask may be lined on the inside with soft cloth to provide greater comfort for the wearer.

Using Wire

Use coat-hanger wire or other heavy yet flexible wire to fashion the basic outline of a mask. Coated electrical wire works well. Wind masking tape tightly around the overlapped joints. Bend additional wire to fashion details such as eyes and ears, and attach to the basic outline shape with thinner binding wire; florists' wire or multicolored telephone wire will do. Again, completely cover the exposed wire joints with masking tape. Next, apply laminae of opaque paper or tissues (colored tissues provide a translucent quality) using diluted glue as an adhesive. (See Laminating Paper, pages 110 to 113.) Allow to dry, and decorate as desired.

Casting

All paper casting begins with the formation of a sheet of paper, so beginning experiments with casting will give you first-hand experience with the paper-making process.

The casting technique allows for great creativity with inexpensive supplies and commonplace appliances, such as the kitchen blender. The process begins with fiber—either cotton linters (a dry, ready-to-use, preprocessed pulp made from cotton, wood or abaca) or paper to be recycled (such as printmaking, drawing or calligraphy paper). The fiber is hydrated by beating with water in a blender or with a special beating and hydrating machine, known as a hydropulper. Color may be added to the resulting pulp, if desired.

In papermaking, the pulp is scooped out of the water solution with a framing system known as a mold and deckle. The mold can be purchased or made by stapling window screening to a simple wooden frame. The deckle is merely an open frame that rests on the mold during paper formation to define the edges of each sheet of paper. Together the mold and deckle act as a sieve, allowing water to pass through the fine-mesh screen and leaving only a thin layer of pulp. The thin sheet is transferred to an absorbent surface, pressed (to remove excess water), and allowed to dry.

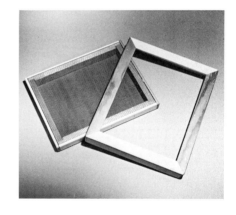

Mold and deckle. The mold is a frame constructed from kiln-dried lumber and covered with aluminum (or heat-shrinking polyester) screen. The deckle (the outer frame) is made from similar wood and fits over the mold during paper formation.

Jean LaPointe Mihalcheon, *Hopak Dancer*, 1991. Cast paper, 24 x 30" (61 x 76 cm). Courtesy the artist.

Casting Sculptural Forms

Sheets of handmade paper can be manipulated during the drying process to produce interesting and dynamic three-dimensional forms. After forming a sheet of handmade paper, let it drain and set for at least one hour on an absorbent base (Pellon fabric or a sheet of commercially-available paper will do). Carefully check one end of the sheet by bending a corner. If the pulp does not slide off, crack or break, it is ready for further manipulation. Pick up the base sheet and gently drape it over or press it into pre-arranged waterproof objects or forms. The objects serve as a mold. Allow the formed pulp to remain on the mold until all parts are completely dry. The piece will retain the shape of the mold.

An electric drill fitted with a paint-stirrer attachment is used to mix the prepared pulp with hot water to form an applesauce-like consistency.

The mold, dipped and raised from the slurry, acquires an even layer of pulp. The deckle was not used in this instance.

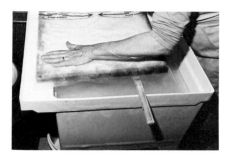

A plastic sheet cut to fit is placed over the pulp. The surface is gently pressed to expel water.

The pulp is released from the mold onto a table.

A cloth is placed over the pulp and lightly rolled to compress the surface and absorb more water. The pulp-forming procedure is repeated to produce the required number of sheets. The wet sheets are kept between layers of plastic until ready for use.

The pulp is inverted into the plaster mold. The protective plastic sheets are removed and the pulp is gently pressed into the mold. The process is repeated; additional sheets are pressed into the mold, each overlapping slightly, until the mold's surface is covered.

A cloth is placed over the pulp and pressed to force the pulp against the mold's surface and absorb additional moisture.

Pressure from auxiliary tools, such as a rolling pin or other rounded wood forms, is applied to the pulp to further compress it.

After drying in the mold for twenty-four hours, the casting is removed. Photo series courtesy of Jean LaPointe Mihalcheon.

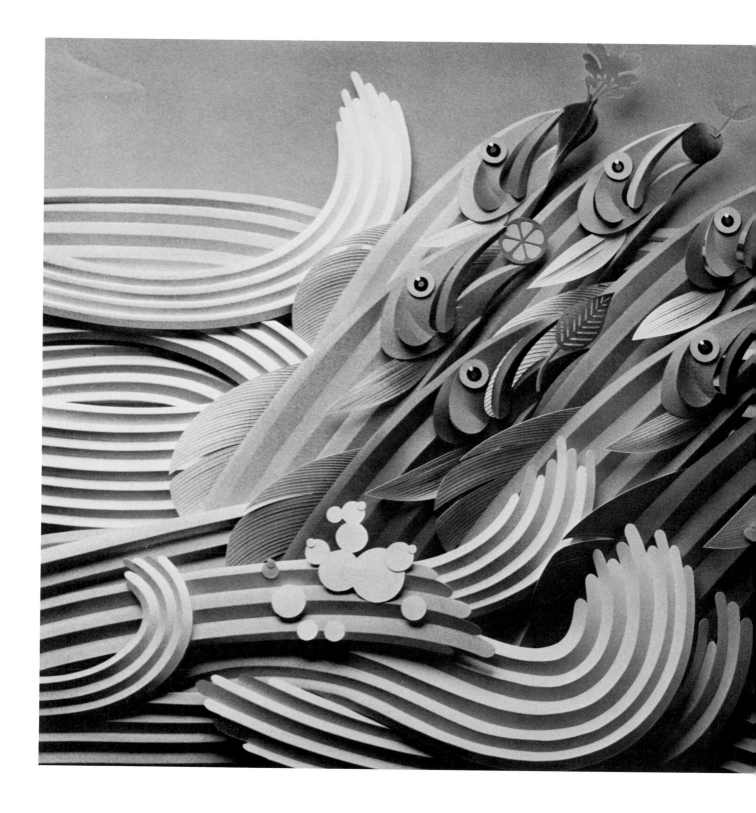

5
Portfolio:
Across
Boundaries

Leo Monahan, *Salmon Run.* Paper, airbrushed color. Courtesy the artist.

Concepts, ideas, visions and dreams—coupled with artistic techniques and skills—give the paper medium its life. When the ideas, technical skills and compositional modes function in concert, there is a wondrous result, integrating thought, action and output. Contemporary papermaker Michael Ponce de Leon put it well when he said, "A work of art is like a gong and hammer—craft, materials and tools in one hand and vision and ideas in the other. By themselves they are mere potentials, but when we strike them together in a single moment of totality, we can experience a profound reverberation."

The following portfolio presents a variety of paper works by artists and students from many parts of the world. Although there is a diversity of works, they represent but a fraction of the rich manifold of styles and techniques by contemporary paper artists. "Today, the emancipation of paper is no longer new," writes critic Jasia Reichart. "What is new is the fact that artists use it so unselfconsciously that the case for paper as a medium needs neither apology nor explanation."

Paper is a user-friendly material that encourages creativity; its potential as an art medium is virtually limitless. "Its beauty," writes artist Joan Packham, "is due in part to its fragility; its strength lies in the ideas that people put into it."

The malleable nature of paper in pulp form allows for the manipulation of surface and structure as well as the integration of mixed media. Marea Atkinson, *The Spectator Series* (detail), 1987–1989. Pulp and mixed media, 28 x 19½ x 5½" (71 x 50 x 14 cm). Courtesy the artist.

Collage. Leo Monahan, *Masks.* Paper, airbrushed color. Courtesy the artist.

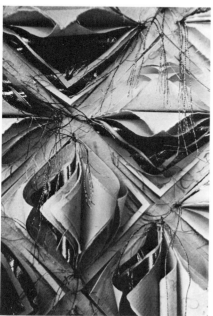

Lynne McElhaney, *Interaction Series* (detail). Paper construction. Courtesy the artist.

Ulrich Hanisch, *Untitled*. Cardboard.
Courtesy Elisabeth Sinken.

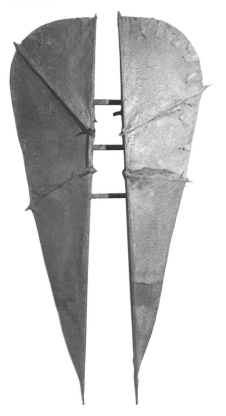

Isabelle Leduc, *Pointe,* 1988. Paper and wood, 56 x 36½" (142 x 93 cm). Courtesy the artist.

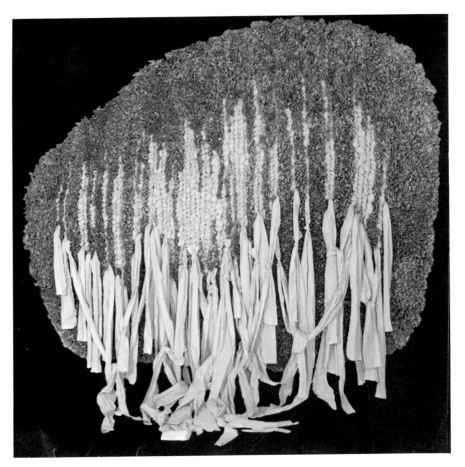

According to the artist Myung-Hee Oh, more than just paper fibers are woven into this wall relief: "Many letters are hidden in the woven fibers; they whisper about beautiful ancient times." Myung-Hee Oh, *Divine Spiritual Trees,* 1990. Korean paper, cotton, 96 x 82½" (250 x 210 cm). Courtesy the artist.

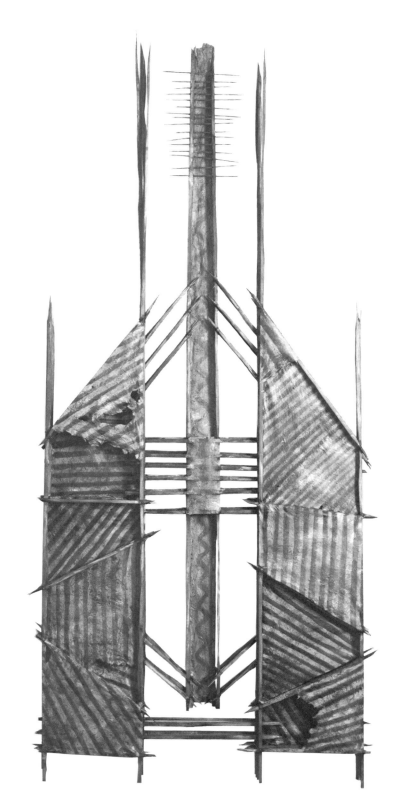

Isabelle Leduc, *Object*, 1984. Handmade paper, wood. Courtesy the artist.

Opposite:
Installation, Anchorage Museum of History and Art. Karen Stahlecker, *Between Eden and Armageddon,* 1989. Handmade paper (kozo, mitsumata, abaca), pigment, wood, fiber, mixed media, 22 x 28 x 68' (6.7 x 8.5 x 20.7 m). Courtesy the artist. Photo by Al Sanders.

Origami designs, such as that of this mobile, are folded into figures or objects without any cutting or gluing. Directions for folding origami designs can be found in books listed in the bibliography. Florence Temko, *Japanese Crane*, 1990. Paper. Courtesy the artist.

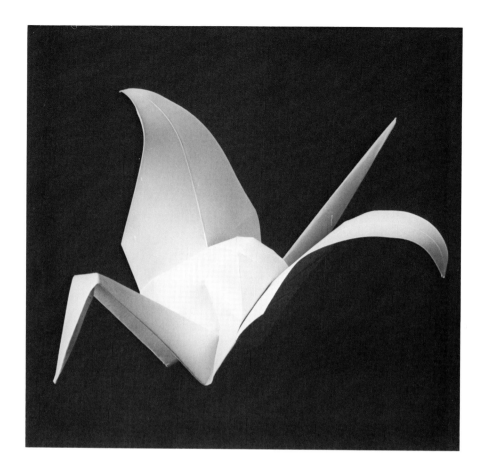

Lise Landry, *La Sorciere Etait En Blanc*, 1982. Woven and sewn Japanese paper, 41 x 26" (105 x 66 cm). Courtesy the artist. Photograph by Gilles St. Pierre.

128

Susan Lyman, *Untitled,* 1982. Reed, bamboo, Nepalese paper, paint, 75 x 70 x 55" (191 x 178 x 140 cm). Courtesy the artist.

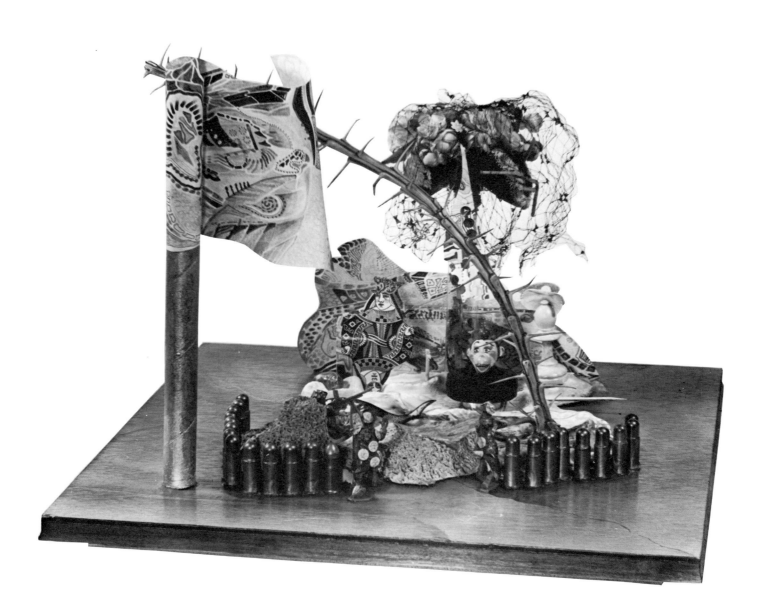

Beate Hoffmeister, *Wheel*, 1967. Paper.
Courtesy Elisabeth Sinken.

Reviva Regev, *Soft and Hard,* 1987. Cast
paper on wood construction and stone,
31½ x 43 x 23½" (80 x 110 x 60 cm).
Courtesy the artist.

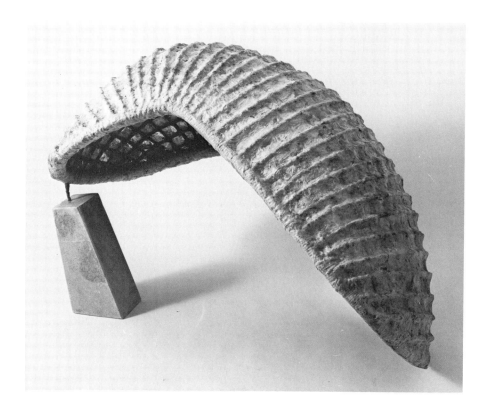

Collage. Teresa Olabuenaga, *La Muñeca Que Nunca Me Regalaron,* 1990. Amate and kozo paper, 20½ x 36½" (52 x 93 cm). Courtesy the artist.

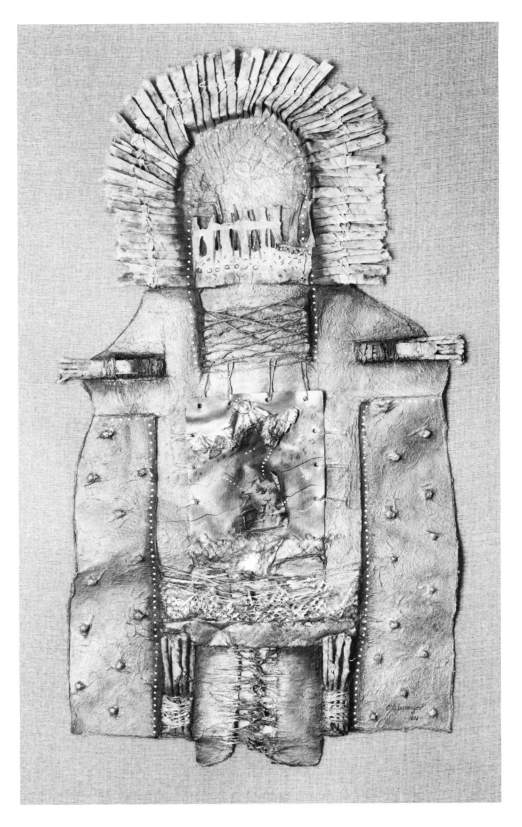

Karen Trask, *La Vanneuse (The Winnower),* 1989. Cast paper, wood, cheesecloth, polystyrene, 26 x 24 x 19½" (67 x 61 x 50 cm). Courtesy the artist.

The understructure for this sculpture was constructed of wire mesh, then covered with many layers of torn paper strips soaked in polymer emulsion. When dry, an undercoat of acrylic gesso was applied and the surface painted. Pat Strakowski, *Picasso Head,* 1991. Papier-mâché, acrylic color, 20 x 8" (51 x 20 cm). Courtesy the artist.

Origami. Florence Temko, *The Bremen Town Musicians,* 1985. Paper and wire. Courtesy the artist.

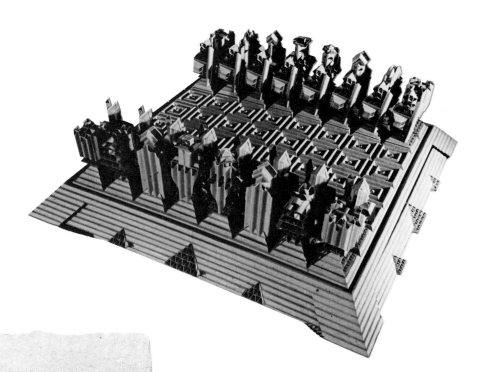

Dennis Humphries, *Chess Set*, 1983.
Corrugated cardboard. Courtesy the
artist.

Cast sculpture. Frank Gallo, *Verity*, 1987.
Handmade paper (abaca and cotton
linter), 24 x 17 x 2" (61 x 43 x 5 cm).
Courtesy the artist.

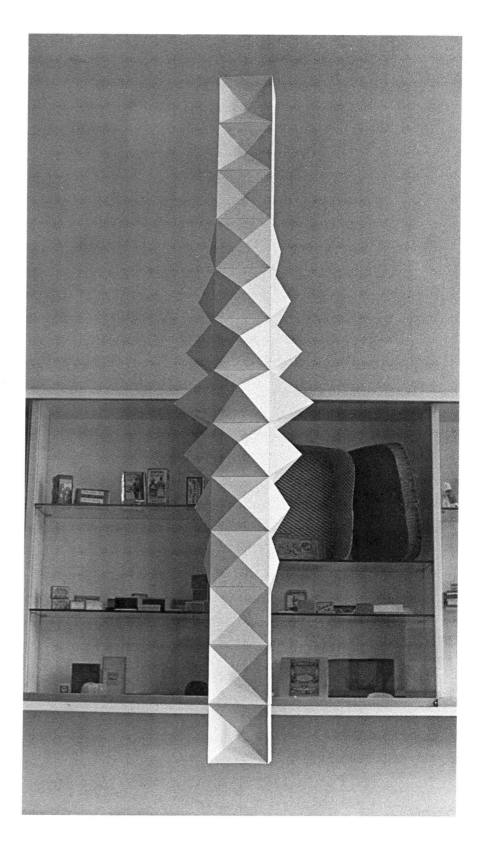

Creased and folded construction. Franz Zeier, *Column (Cube to Star Transformation)*, 1974. Paper. Courtesy the artist.

Brian Gladwell, *Desk,* 1990. Cardboard, fiberboard, lacquer, 32 x 65 x 28" (81 x 165 x 71 cm). Courtesy Susan Whitney Gallery, Regina, Saskatchewan.

Lilian A. Bell, *Revolving Door Policy,* 1990. Cast paper, 59 x 44 x 26" (150 x 112 x 66 cm). Courtesy the artist.

Tom Holland, *Free Standing Paper 40,* 1981. Paper, epoxy, 45¼ x 23 x 14" (115 x 58 x 36 cm). Courtesy John Berggruen Gallery, San Francisco.

Newspaper and brown paper are laminated with white glue, then applied over a clay sculpture. Billy Nicholas, *Archbishop Mask* (detail). Papier-mâché (layer method), color, varnish, gold powder, 20 x 46" (50 cm x 118 cm). Courtesy the artist.

Bill Laing, *Berlin Still Life,* 1990. Silkscreen and paper collage, 5" high (13 cm). Courtesy the artist.

Carolyn Dahl, *Sky Signals.* Pulp, color, 9 x 15 x 15" (23 x 38 x 38 cm). Courtesy the artist.

Stage-set format. Lois Polansky, *Indian Theatre Tableau*, 1990. 37 x 59 x 5" (94 x 150 x 13 cm). Courtesy the artist.

This artist works in a technique he calls "free-casting," shaping the paper pulp entirely by hand rather than casting into a mold. This method tends to be slow and deliberate, layering pulp in various areas of the work, and a single piece may take days or weeks to complete. John Babcock, *Descending Angel*. Handmade paper, 47 x 48" (119 x 122 cm). Courtesy the artist.

Pavlos, *Boulevard des Batignolles I*, 1986.
Paper collage, 76 x 77" (193 x 195 cm).
Courtesy Redmann Galerie, Berlin.

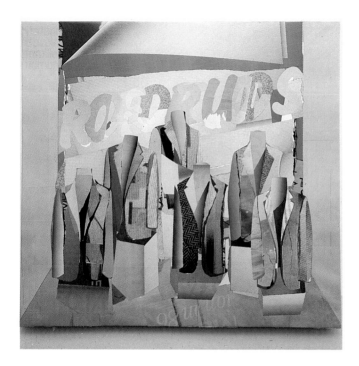

Arndt von Diepenbroick, *Flying Dragon
(The Dream of Flying Series)*, 1987. Paper,
bamboo, wood, 2½ x 4 x 4' (.8 x 1.2 x 1.2 m).
Courtesy the artist.

Wall light. Louise Vergette, *Figure*, 1989.
Papier-mâché, glass, 33½ x 32" (85 x
82 cm). Courtesy the artist.

Stitched and sewn collage. Lise Landry, *Offrande,* 1989. Paper, acrylic paint, 54 x 54" (138 x 138 cm). Courtesy the artist.

Pavlos, *Bar,* 1972. Paper, Plexiglas, 17¾ x 33½ x 7" (45 x 85 x 18 cm). Courtesy Redmann Galerie, Berlin.

Dan Reeder, *Twirp and Troll.* Papier-mâché. Courtesy the artist.

Kyoko Ibe, *White Crystal* (installation), 1988. Washi paper, mirrors. Courtesy the artist.

Alexandra Soteriou, *Blue Rondel.* Cast handmade paper, 48 x 44" (122 x 112 cm). Courtesy the artist.

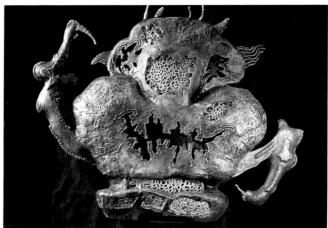

Billy Nicholas, *Cut-Head #2*, 1990. Papier-mâché. Courtesy the artist.

Collage. Graceann Warn, *Domaine,* 1991. Paper, fabric, wood, string, acrylic color, chalk. Courtesy the artist.

Book format. Colleen Barry-Wilson, *Tropical Journal,* 1990. Paper, mixed media, 15 x 30 x 4" (38 x 76 x 10 cm). Courtesy the artist.

Patricia Nix, *Toy Shop,* 1979. Paper, mixed media, 12 x 12 x 2½" (30 x 30 x 6 cm). Collection National Museum of American Art, Smithsonian Institute, Washington, D.C. Courtesy the artist.

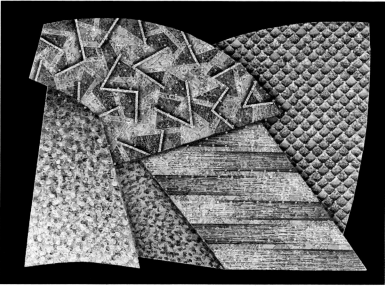

View of Arndt Von Diepenbroick's studio, 1991. Papier-mâché figures. Courtesy the artist. Photo by Helga Sittl.

Glenn Brill, *On the Carpet,* 1988. Woven paper, dyed silk, mixed media, 30 x 40" (76 x 102 cm). Courtesy the artist.

Collage. Teresa Olabuenaga, *Sobre el Sexo y la Fragilidad*, 1991. Amate, kozo, 24 x 40 x 24" (60 x 100 x 60 cm). Courtesy the artist.

Red Grooms, *Gertrude*, 1975. Colored
lithograph on Arches cover paper, cut
out, glued and mounted in a Plexiglas
box, 19¼ x 22 x 10" (49 x 56 x 25 cm),
edition of 46. Courtesy Brooke Alexander,
Inc., New York.

Arndt von Diepenbroick, *Fantasy Birds,*
1989. Papier-mâché. Courtesy the artist.

The artist produced this sculpture by first
carving "boulders" of Styrofoam. Pulp
was applied over the Styrofoam, then
pressed with a sponge to extract water.
(The Styrofoam remains within the
sculpture.) The surface was given a patina
of acrylic paint, black india ink, sand
mixed with acrylic color and Fleckstone
(an imitation-granite spray paint). Lilian
A. Bell, *My Destination is a New Point of
Departure,* 1989. Cast paper (made from
mulberry fibers and European hemp),
Styrofoam, color, 14 x 19 x 19" (36 x 48 x 48
cm). Photo by Glenn Hashitani.

Charles Hilger, *Untitled,* 1988. Handmade
cast paper, 49 x 49" (124 x 124 cm).
Courtesy the artist.

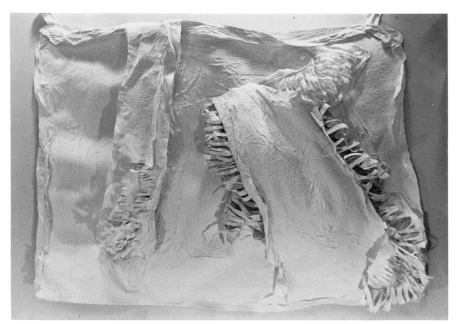

Octopus. Paper sculpture from the
author's design workshop, The University
of Calgary.

Maria Panagosis, *Open Cube,* 1987.
Cardboard, colored string, 15 x 15 x 15"
(38 x 38 x 38 cm). Courtesy the artist.

Colleen Barry, *The Cinderella Shrine*, 1990. Paper, mixed media, 26 x 12 x 12" (66 x 30 x 30 cm). Courtesy the artist.

Book object. Takashi Hayashi, *Concerning the Letter "L,"* 1974. Kent paper, 150 x 30 x 15" (381 x 76 x 38 cm). Courtesy Museum of Contemporary Art, Montreal.

What's a book?
Everything or nothing.
The eye that sees it is all.

RALPH WALDO EMERSON, NINETEENTH CENTURY AMERICAN WRITER

Blowfish. Paper sculpture from the design
workshop, Alberta College of Art, Calgary.
Courtesy Ken Samuelson.

Carol Rosen, *Intuitions and Boundaries IX*. Paper, wood, grass, 79 x 105 x 13" (201 x 267 x 33 cm). Courtesy the artist. Photo by D. James Dee.

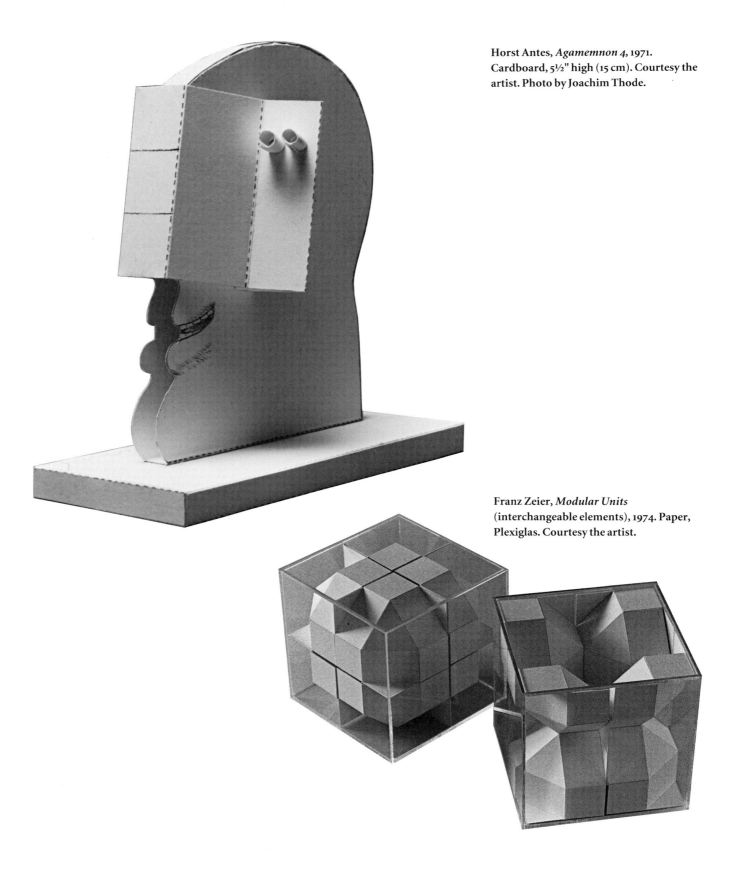

Horst Antes, *Agamemnon 4,* 1971.
Cardboard, 5½" high (15 cm). Courtesy the
artist. Photo by Joachim Thode.

Franz Zeier, *Modular Units*
(interchangeable elements), 1974. Paper,
Plexiglas. Courtesy the artist.

Appendix

Simple Papermaking

(Prepared in consultation with Sheril Cunning, papermaker and author.)

Papermaking provides a special bonus for the craftsperson: the opportunity to create the art medium itself. This handmade paper can then be used to explore further dimensions in paper sculpture.

For simple papermaking, you'll need the following supplies:

- Household blender
- Fiber (cotton linters, abaca or paper to be recycled, such as printmaking or drawing paper)
- Mold and deckle (approximately 6" x 8", made from a window screen or purchased from a papermaking supplier)
- Vat (laundry or dishwashing tub)
- Pellon (a thin fabric interfacing, not the iron-on type)
- Measuring cups
- Work area (table and floor not susceptible to water damage)
- Two small buckets
- Plastic sieve
- Sponge (preferably a natural sea sponge)
- Absorbant cloth (terrycloth towels or wool blankets)
- Mop (for floor wipe-ups)
- Tray or area for drying papers

Procedure

1. Select the fiber to be used. Paper pulp can be made in two ways: by recycling paper, or with pre-processed fiber. If you choose to recycle paper, use a good quality drawing or printmaking paper that contains little or no sizing. Do not use watercolor paper. Ready-to-use fiber (cotton linters or abaca) may be purchased from papermaking suppliers.

2. Prepare the fiber. Cut the fiber (paper, linters or abaca sheets) into 4" squares and soak it in a bucket of water for a few minutes.

3. Prepare the work area by placing several towels or blankets on a work table. Provide space for three steps of the papermaking process: sheet formation, transfer of newly-formed sheets and drying. Place a vat for the pulp on the towels and keep a small bucket on hand to hold extra pulp.

4. Fill the jar of the blender with water, allowing 1" or 2" at the top for pulp. Use one 4" square of soaked linters or abaca or two 4" squares of soaked light-weight drawing paper for each blender container. Tear the wet squares into ¾" pieces, put them in the blender and beat at a slow to medium speed. Beat paper for one minute, linters or abaca for two minutes. (Note: Never attempt to macerate old rags or cotton balls in the blender.) Pour the beaten pulp (slurry) into the vat and bucket. Make several batches of pulp to fill both the vat and the extra bucket. Cotton linters and abaca will produce a thicker pulp than recycled paper; add water to thin the pulp to a creamy consistency, if necessary. The first few paper sheets formed will be fairly thick and consume a lot of the original pulp from the vat. Replenish the vat with pulp from the extra bucket after three or four papers are formed. To do so, scoop pulp out of the reserve bucket with a sieve and transfer it to the vat; stir well before forming additional sheets.

A household blender is the only machine necessary for simple papermaking.

5. Dip the mold and deckle into the pulp. First place the deckle on top of the mold on the side closest to the screening. Then, while holding the mold and deckle firmly together, dip the framing system into the slurry vertically. At the bottom of the vat, level the mold and deckle beneath the surface of the pulp and raise it straight up and out of the vat. It is important that the mold and deckle be held flat as it is raised out of the slurry. Immediately after removing the mold and deckle from the vat, gently shake it from side to side and front to back, allowing the fibers to settle. (If the sheet does not form well, turn the screen upside down and shake the pulp back into the vat. Don't rub or wad up the pulp; wadded pulp will not go back into solution in the vat.)

6. Remove the deckle and quickly transfer the newly-formed paper from the screen to a piece of Pellon fabric that is at least 1" larger than the sheet of paper on all sides. To do so, hold one edge of the mold down on an edge of the Pellon cloth. In one continuous movement, quickly roll the mold down flat on the Pellon and up again on its opposite edge. This action will release the paper onto the cloth. This process is known as couching (pronounced COO-ching). Place a second piece of Pellon on top of the paper. You have produced a Pellon-paper-Pellon "sandwich."

7. Press the paper. Stack the Pellon-paper-Pellon sandwiches between two pieces of thick plywood. Weigh down the plywood with cement blocks or other heavy items for about ten minutes. Remove each sandwich and place it on a flat surface to dry.

8. Air dry. Because paper dries more by evaporation than by heat, it's best to let the newly-formed sheets dry naturally. You can iron them dry, but this may cause curling; even air drying may make paper warp. To flatten the sheets, remove the Pellon (it will easily peel away from the paper) and weigh down the sheet with a book or board.

Adding color and texture

There are several ways to add color to handmade paper. Aqueous-dispersed pigments made especially for papermaking are available from papermaking suppliers. They are easy to use and produce rich and vibrant color. Alternatively, dried flower petals (such as carnations, calendulas, geraniums and freesia), cut-up bits of yarn, thread, ribbons or fabric, and confetti or glitter can be added to the vat of pulp fiber. (Do not put these items in the blender.) Colorful Canson or Japanese Moriki papers can be used also; recycle them with water in the blender and mix them with the pulp in the vat. To obtain pastel shades, mix a few scraps of colored paper with the fiber when it is first being prepared, and beat in the blender.

To add texture to handmade paper, you can replace the top layer of Pellon in the Pellon-paper-Pellon sandwich with bamboo mats, straw broom bristles, twigs, textured fabrics or other textured surfaces. Press down lightly with a sponge and leave the textured material on the paper until it is dry.

For additional information on papermaking, consult books listed in the bibliography.

Sources of Supplies

Japanese papers
Aiko's Art Materials
714 North Wabash Avenue
Chicago, IL 60611

Custom-made molds, deckles
Edwin Amies & Sons, Ltd.
33 Amsbury Road
Coxheath, NR Maidstone, Kent
ME1740P England

Papers
Andrews/Nelson/Whitehead
31-10 48th Avenue
Long Island City, NY 11101

Papers
Bienfang, Division of Hunt
 Manufacturing
230 South Broad Street
Philadelphia, PA 19102

Art materials
Brault & Bouthillier
700 Beaumont
Montreal, Quebec
H3N lV5 Canada

*Papermaking supplies, pulps, fibers,
colorants, molds, deckles*
Carriage House
1 Fitchburg Street
Somerville, MA 02143

Papers, cardboard
Crescent Cardboard
100 Werst Willow Road
Wheeling, IL 60090

Papers
Crestwood Paper
315 Hudson Street
New York, NY 10013

Papermaking supplies, pulp, linters, fibers
Dieu Donne Papermill
3 Crosby Street
New York, NY 10013

*Papermaking supplies, pulp, hydropulpers,
equipment, pigments*
Gold's Artworks
2100 North Pine Street
Lumberton, NC 28358

Papers, art supplies
M. Grumbacher, Inc.
460 West 34th Street
New York, NY 10001

Papers, art supplies
Heinz Jordan
900 Magnetic Drive
Downsview, Ontario
MEJ 2C4 Canada

Papermaking supplies
Kakali Handmade Papers
1249 Cartwright Street
Granville Island
Vancouver, British Columbia
V6H 3R7 Canada

*Papermaking supplies, equipment, pulp,
custom papers*
Magnolia Editions
2527 Magnolia Street
Oakland, CA 94607

*Papermaking supplies, equipment, pulp,
fiber, colorants*
Lee Scott McDonald
P.O. Box 264
Charlestown, MA 02129

Papers
Morilla Company
211 Bowers Street
Holyoke, MA 01040

*Arts and crafts supplies, papers, paints,
tools, equipment*
Nasco
901 Janesville Avenue
Fort Atkinson, WI 53530

Handmade papers
New York Central Art Supply
62 Third Avenue
New York, NY 10003

Imported papers
Oriental Art Supply
10181 Crailet Drive
Huntington Beach, CA 92646

Handmade papers
Paper Source
1506 West 12th Street
Los Angeles, CA 90015

*Arts and crafts supplies, papers, molds,
kits, pulp*
Pyramid Art Supply
P.O. Box 877
Urbana, IL 61801-0877

Handmade papers
Daniel Smith Artist Materials
4130 First Avenue South
Seattle, WA 98134

Papers
Special Papers, Inc.
P.O. Box 643
Wilton, CT 06897

Papers
Strathmore Paper Company
South Broad Street
Westfield, MA 01085

Papers
Tara Materials, Inc.
111 Fredrix Alley
Lawrenceville, GA 30246

*Papermaking supplies, pulp, fibers,
pigments, chemicals, equipment*
Twinrocker Equipment Company
110 Third Street
P.O. Box 246
Brookston, IN 47923

Papers
Utrecht Manufacturing Company
33 35th Street
Brooklyn, NY 11232

Papers, art supplies
Winsor & Newton
555 Winsor Drive
Secaucus, NJ 07094

Imported papers
Yasutomo & Company
235 Valley Drive
Brisbane, CA 94005

Bibliography

Ballinger, Raymond, *Design with Paper.* New York: Van Nostrand Reinhold, 1982.

Barret, Timothy, *Japanese Papermaking: Traditions, Tools and Techniques.* New York: Weatherhill, 1983.

Bawden, Juliet, *The Art and Craft of Papier Mâché.* New York: Grove Weidenfeld, 1989.

Bell, Lilian A., *Plant Fibers for Paper Making.* McMinnville, OR: Lilliacae Press, 1984.

Bell, Lilian A., *Papyrus, Tapa, Amate and Rice Paper: Papermaking in Africa, The Pacific, Latin America and Southeast Asia.* McMinnville, OR: Lilliacae Press, 1985.

Boyes, Janet, *Making Paper Costumes.* Boston: Plays, 1974.

Chatani, Masahiro. *Paper Magic: Pop-Up Craft.* Tokyo: Ondorisha, 1988.

Cunning, Sheril, *Handmade Paper: A Practical Guide to Oriental And Western Techniques.* Escondido, CA: Ravens's World Press, 1989.

Elderfield, John, *The Cut-Outs of Henri Matisse.* New York: George Braziller, 1978.

Grater, Michael, *Creative Paper Toys and Crafts.* New York: Dover Publications, 1981.

Heller, Jules, *Papermaking.* New York: Watson-Guptill, 1978.

Hunter, Dard, *Papermaking: The History and Techniques of an Ancient Craft.* New York: Dover Publications, 1978.

Johnston, Mary Grace, *Paper Sculpture.* Worcester, MA: Davis Publications, Inc., 1964

Koretsy, Elaine, *Color for the Handpapermaker.* Brookline, MA: Carriage House Press, 1982.

Leisure, Jerry, *Understanding Three Dimensions.* New Jersey: Prentice-Hall, 1987.

Leopold-Hoesch Museum, *International Biennial of Paper Art* (catalogs). Duren, Germany: Leopold-Hoesch Museum, 1986, 1988, 1990.

Miyazaki, Koji, *An Adventure in Multidimensional Space.* New York: John Wiley & Sons, 1983.

Ogami, Hiroshi, *Forms in Paper.* New York: Van Nostrand Reinhold, 1971.

Pearce, Peter, *Structure in Nature is a Strategy for Design.* Cambridge, MA: Massachusetts Institute of Technology Press, 1980.

Qualley, Charles A., *Safety in the Artroom.* Worcester, MA: Davis Publications, Inc., 1986.

Rottger, Ernst, *Creative Paper Design.* New York: Van Nostrand Reinhold, 1962.

Rush, Peter, *Papier Mâché.* New York: Farrar Straus Giroux, 1980.

Seitz, William C., *The Art of Assemblage.* New York: Museum of Modern Art, 1961.

Shannon, Faith, *Paper Pleasures.* New York: Weidenfeld & Nicolson, 1987.

Streeter, Tal, *The Art of the Japanese Kite.* New York: Weatherhill, 1974.

Temko, Florence, *Paper Pandas and Jumping Frogs: Origami and its Uses.* San Francisco: China Books, 1986.

Temko, Florence, *Made with Paper.* London: Dragon's World, 1991.

Toale, Bernard, *The Art of Papermaking.* Worcester, MA: Davis Publications, Inc., 1983.

Webb, Sheila, *Paper, The Continuous Thread.* Cleveland, OH: Cleveland Museum of Art, 1982.

Wong, Wucius, *Principles of Three-Dimensional Design.* New York: Van Nostrand Reinhold, 1977.

Yamada, Sadami, *New Dimensions in Paper Craft.* Tokyo: Japan Publications, 1966.

Zeier, Franz, *Paper Constructions.* New York: Charles Scribner's Sons, 1980.

Index